VOLUME FOUR

Collected Stories

Edited by Elizabeth Beck, Christina Butcher, Christian Carvajal, Jackie Fender, Daniel Person, and Joshua Swainston

Copyright © 2017 by Creative Colloquy

Cover art by Bismark Pinera
Cover design by Christina Butcher

Creative Colloquy
Tacoma, WA
www.CreativeColloquy.com

ISBN-13: 978-1979536172
ISBN-10: 1979536171

To Creative Colloquy's fans and family.

Creative (kree-ey-tiv) – adjective: having the quality or power of creating resulting from originality of thought, expression, etc.

+

Colloquy (kol-uh-kwee) – noun: a conversational exchange; dialogue, a conference.

=

Creative Colloquy – community: literary site and review AKA word nerds and storytellers gathering upon pages, cyberspace and in person to share their prose.

Table of Contents

Greetings Dear Readers,

We gather here on the page once again to present our fourth print collection. As you flip through the pages you hold in your hands, we hope you'll discover something that whispers sweet nothings in your ear, elicits a giggle and guffaw, or resonates at the core of your being.

Via a blind submission process, the Creative Colloquy team has pored over each story, letting the prose marinate in our brain space so that we could carefully consider each piece of work. Our aim was to curate a word journey, an ebb and flow of expression that serves as a narrative of the human condition. Each invoking a muse of the myriad of feelings and thoughts we may have experienced in life.

The collection is not simply a word journey but a matrimony of the written word and art. Each short story or poem is accompanied with a visual representation, crafted by south sound artists. Contributing artists were given complete creative freedom when translating the written word into a partnering piece of art using their medium of choice. By allowing this creative freedom and using a blind submission process we hope to display the diversity of our local literary culture and to support our storytellers that have so willfully allowed themselves to dive deep and subject themselves to the vulnerable creative process.

Creative Colloquy strives to provide a safety net for creative risk. We gather in cafes over roasted bean concoctions and craft beer. We connect online, words swirling through our pixelated screens to share the written word and here on the page. We do this out of an admiration of the written word, and a deep desire to share South Sound scribes' unique narratives; to provide a space where storytellers can use their voice to weave threads of prose from their daydreams to our ready eyes and hearts.

It is CC's sincere hope you find snippets of escape, adventure and even raw truths among these pages.

Warmest Regards,
Jackie

Five Six Seven Eight
by
Linda Norlander

You came to my hospital ward in the middle of my shift just before Hannah, the aide working with me, went home sick. We were busy, short-staffed, and I told the charge nurse I couldn't take another patient. She shrugged and said, "Sorry."

I remembered you as younger, your dark hair pulled back into a shining, tight bun. You had the same thin face, but now your cheeks were sunken and your hair was yellow-gray and close-cropped. I said to you, "Ms. Martha. What a surprise." You peered at me for a long time with those piercing, blue eyes of yours before you said, "Nurse, get me another pillow. This one is too hard."

You once danced with the Rockettes in New York and in a showgirl revue at the Riviera in Las Vegas. When your joints wore down and your kick wasn't so high, you moved back to Farmland, the small town from which we both came. You taught phys ed to the Farmland children and coached the high-school dance line.

I was a short, chubby student. My muscles were stiff and inflexible, and I was clumsy. I stumbled, tripped and fell on a regular basis. After I tumbled down a flight of stairs and broke my wrist, my mother insisted I join the dance line. She thought it would help.

I had high hopes. I'd seen the movies *Dirty Dancing* and *Footloose*. The girls leapt and twirled with grace and awe. They had happy endings.

Despite my miserable tryout you took me on as your project, telling my mother you could fix that clumsiness. You told us it was about timing and knowing your right from your left. "Get the rhythm, get the time, and you can dance."

I believed you.

While Becky Torvald could do the splits and Ramona Baker could do a back handspring, I could do a brush-kick-step only by staring at my feet.

"Heads up," you'd yell, banging your walking stick on the gym floor. "Chin up." You'd stop in front of me and bang your stick again. "Other foot."

The more you yelled, the more you used me as an example for the team on how not to do it, the more I tried. I would go home every night and practice. I'd pirouette in front of the television and stumble into the sofa. I'd bang my shins on the coffee table and twirl until I thought I'd throw up.

After three weeks, you took me aside for a serious talk. You said, "I can't make you a great dance-line dancer. I'm not even sure I can make you a good dance-line dancer. But by God, I can make you a better dance-line dancer."

I didn't know you'd stolen those lines from the movie *All That Jazz*. I believed you were a poet.

Four weeks later, on Columbus Day, you finally threw in the towel. I remember it well because for the first time in Farmland High School history the school didn't have a day off. In the past, we closed for Columbus Day weekend, not to celebrate the man who discovered an island in the Caribbean but because it was the opening of pheasant-hunting season. The principal and all the male teachers would head to the cornfields to blast the poor birds. But that year, we had a rare shortage of pheasants, and school stayed open. I heard later the pheasants got a virus and that's why they disappeared.

As it turned out, on Columbus Day I myself wished for a virus and chance to disappear. We were rehearsing for our first competition with nearby Renville. Renville won the district every year and you, Ms. Martha, decided to change that. You stood in front of us and said, "It's timing. It's always timing." When the music started, you thumped your stick on the gym floor.

Five, six, seven, eight …

So now you were here, on my ward with thirty other sick people and not enough staff. I was the dancer and choreographer making sure the meds got passed, the IVs didn't run dry and no one fell out of bed. I could give you all the care you needed. I could coordinate the treatments, the medicine, the turning and bathing. I could finally dance for you.

As I tucked the new pillow under your head, I leaned down to ask you if you were comfortable. I saw a look of repulsion as you whispered, "Honey, take that smock off. You have blood on it."

It was a splotch, a mere dab of blood from the IV start in room 232, but you waved me away like you used to when I couldn't catch the beat.

Five, six, seven, eight …

Back then, you counted and gave us our cues, and I urged my pudgy, little body on. But when you said to go left, my legs went right and when you said leap, my feet stayed firmly on the ground.

During a break, Cindy Lord, soon to be my former best friend, glared at me and muttered, "Clumsy oaf. You can't keep time." I stepped on her toe the very next set and nearly broke it.

After rehearsal, you called me out. "Come, sit." Even though you were old and kind of wrinkly, you could still sit cross-legged with your knees touching the floor.

"Honey, I can't make you a great dancer and I can't make you good dancer and it's finally clear to me, I can't even make you a better dancer. What I can do is make you team manager."

At least you were honest.

Dreams of backhand springs and pirouettes and high kicks were smashed that Columbus Day. I felt like one of the Caribbean islanders who discovered Columbus brought, not only shiny trinkets, but also measles and smallpox. I would be the towel person who got to stand at the side while Becky and Cindy and Ramona high-kicked and marched to "Gonna Fly Now."

After that, I carried water and sewed on buttons and sequins and sprayed a lot of hair. I didn't tell Mother I'd been kicked off the team for incompetence until our first competition. When she learned I wasn't in the dance line she just shrugged and said, "Oh, well, maybe you should try out for basketball next year."

But I discovered one thing about you in those days leading up to our competition with Renville. I learned you, the Rockette and Las Vegas showgirl, couldn't stand the sight of blood.

I grew up on a farm. I knew the rhythm of life. Blood didn't bother me. Veterinarians were expensive so we sewed up the lambs when they got tangled in the barbed-wire fence. We wrung the chickens' necks and chopped off their heads. We delivered the calves and placentas and mopped up the blood. So, when Becky Torvald high-kicked Ramona Baker in the forehead and split it open, you collapsed and I dabbed the blood from her face and brought you a glass of water and called Ramona's mother to come and get her. The dance team was so busy fussing over both of you that no one thanked me for handling the day. But I figured, maybe I couldn't dance but had the rhythm for taking care of people.

Five, six, seven, eight …

So now as you fussed about the blood on my scrubs and waved me away, the IV pump in room 239 beeped, the light went on in room 241 and a little voice in room 243 cried, "Help! Help!" I was back on the dance line, and I'd lost my rhythm again.

I moved from room to room, fumbling with syringes and pumps and bags of IV fluids. Time swept by, and in the back of my head I heard the cadence of your walking stick on the floor of the gym and it was out of sync with all the work I had to do. When I looked at my watch I was already late with the vitamins to put in your IV and potassium to put in the patient in room 239. I cheated. The hospital-safety policy was specific that nurses did not carry loaded syringes in the pockets of their smocks, but my aide was gone, the floor was out of rhythm and I was late. I remembered distinctly the first day of dance line when you said, "Girls, to be on time is to be late." Well, I was truly late with the meds. I put the potassium for room 239 in my left pocket and your vitamins in my right.

I hurried into your room and you were sitting up in bed, your back ramrod straight. "Nurse, this pillow still isn't right." You sounded testy, the same tone you had for me when the dance line went left and my body went right.

Just as I was getting the line ready to inject, the old guy in room 237 streaked by wearing only a pair of blue hospital slippers, blood running down his arm where he'd pulled out his IV. You saw him and shrieked. I pushed the vitamins in your line without looking at the label on the syringe and ran after his flat, wrinkly ass. I caught him just before he reached the back exit. He batted at me like a kid with a new drum set. By the time I got back to you, my arms were bruised and the light had gone out in your eyes.

You died on my shift amid defibrillators and the rhythm of chest thumps timed to the Bee Gees' "Stayin' Alive." The doctor pronounced you just before my shift was over.

When all the paperwork was done, I sat in the lounge bruised and bloodied, the Bee Gees swimming through my head. I thought about your walking stick and the thudding sound that reverberated across the gym floor. A tear

Art by Amber McLean

dribbled down my cheek and when I reached into my right hand pocket for a tissue, I discovered a full syringe of vitamins.

It was then that I remembered you once said to me, "Honey, you'll be the death of me if you can't figure out your right from your left."

Five, six, seven, eight …

Murpam

by

Drew Piston

Wilson from Commuters was trying to organize a strike or at least a union. He'd buy a round at the Boar and Barrister and gather everyone around, foam on his moustache. What are they going to do, he'd say, replace all of us in the middle of the night? Where would they find that many doppelgangers? As long as we stick together they'll be up a creek. Murpam listened but didn't say anything.

Then one morning there was a new Wilson at the bus stop, with a Russian accent. Murpam kept his head down.

Every night before bed Murpam would write a journal entry in the hardware-store-accounting ledger, always on the first page. He hadn't caught Props and Replacements in the act of replacing it yet, but he also hadn't worked up the nerve to keep it under his pillow instead of on his desk. This night, at the top of page one he wrote: "Days since losing track: 42."

Underneath he wrote: "First change coming my way. Tomorrow, instead of saying, 'What can I do for you?' I'm supposed to say, "How can I help you?""

Usually he would write more than that, but he didn't want to write about the new Russian Wilson and couldn't think of anything else so he tossed it onto his desk, turned out the light and went to sleep.

The next day, though, The Subject didn't come into the store, and Murpam's Morning Memo instructed him to revert to his previously assigned opening dialogue.

The sad fact was The Subject rarely came into the hardware store, which left Murpam with time on his hands. Sure, Diller came in on her lunch break every day to browse, her shock of orange hair a sharp contrast to the shop's drab aisles. But she took her role of Disinterested Bystander much too seriously and rarely even glanced Murpam's way.

So he'd while away his time with a book or a crossword puzzle, all the while hoping and dreading that The Subject would come in.

The recruiter for the job had been a younger man than Murpam, with trendy glasses and tight-fitting pants. He showed up at the community acting school bustling with energy. One of the first things he did was lift up his shirt to show off his six-pack. "I got paid to get these babies," he said. "Best job I've ever had. My uptime was every actor's dream, and my downtime was my own."

He dropped to the floor and whipped off a dozen pushups. "I made myself a better man with that free time, time I was getting paid for," he said. "I exercised. I read. I learned to parlez vouz the français. The ladies dig that." He winked at Murpam, who was well aware he had very little the ladies dug.

Murpam took the bus down to the intake office, a one-room box in a strip mall, intending to just ask some questions. But the spiritless woman behind the desk handed him a form on a clipboard, and after he filled it out he was all signed up.

The first week on the job he was a nervous wreck, peering out the windows to see if he could catch a glimpse of The Subject. They'd given him a big, eight-and-a-half-by-eleven glossy as part of the orientation packet, and on the fifth day Murpam saw him wandering around the street looking haggard and bewildered. It wasn't until the tenth day that The Subject actually entered the shop.

His heart pounding in his chest, Murpam delivered his line: "What can I do for you?" He worked his fingers against his palms, trying to wipe the sweat away.

The Subject spared him a single, suspicious glance, then picked up a two-pack of light bulbs. "How much?" he asked. His nose twitched, sniffing the air.

Murpam had no idea what light bulbs cost, or what anything cost. "Two ninety-nine," he said. The Subject threw some crumpled bills at him and stalked out, which was just as well with Murpam. It took him twenty minutes to figure out how to open the cash register, deposit the bills and throw a cent into the "take a penny, leave a penny" jar.

A week later The Subject returned, wild-eyed and frantic. "What can I do for you?" said Murpam.

"Say something different," whispered The Subject. There was a pleading note to his voice, with an undertone of terror.

"'Something different,'" said Murpam, before he could stop himself. The Subject just stared, so Murpam went back to his bread and butter. "What can I do for you?"

Once, during orientation, Murpam took a wrong turn on his way back from a smoke break and ended up in Props and Replacements. The room was only fifteen feet wide, but so long he could hardly see the end. Dividers were set up every twenty feet or so, labeled with mundane descriptions like "Bus Stop," "Commuters" and "Bookstore." He'd received his assignment that morning, and about a third of the way down was a "Hardware Store" sign. Inside the cubicle he found a mannequin wearing a mustard sweater and tough, dark-brown pants. Behind the mannequin was a clothing rack with fifty more mustard sweaters, exactly the same, and about thirty more pairs of pants. Behind that was a towering stack of cardboard boxes.

He held one sweater up to his chest but there was no mirror to use. The sweater seemed like it would fit okay. He wandered back to the classroom, where the instructor was going over appropriate courses of action if The Subject showed signs of illness or physical injury. "Breaking character = broken contract!" was written on the chalkboard, and above that, "TUESDAY."

Taylor from the bookstore came over every few days with a candy bar and backpack full of detective novels. He'd chew the candy bar while Murpam rifled through to find one he hadn't read yet, only half-listening to Taylor ramble on about his latest crush.

"Miranda," Taylor said last week. "You know, over at the bank." Murpam shrugged noncommittally, which was more than enough participation for Taylor. "She's got this thing she does when she eats." He spread his hands out in front of him, conjuring up a dining table and place setting. "She'll scoop up some pasta or soup or whatever, and halfway to her mouth she'll pause with it and sort of look it over." He inspected the invisible utensil in his miming hand. "Then she sighs, like it's let her down, let her down in some personal and unforgivable way, and puts it in her mouth."

Murpam flipped through a promising paperback with an ivory pawn on the cover. "You watch her eat?" he asked.

"What if I were that forkful?" said Taylor. He lifted himself up to a sitting position on the counter, casting a wistful look out the window. "What I wouldn't give to inspire such disappointment, such acceptance." He put one finger in the air, pedantically. "Reluctant acceptance, true! But acceptance."

Murpam, as usual, could think of nothing worth saying, and feared any attempts to curtail the conversation would have the opposite effect. He zipped up the backpack.

"Do you ever wish it would rain?" asked Taylor.

"Not really," said Murpam.

"I get that it's supposed to be the same day, over and over," said Taylor. "But maybe they could knock The Subject out for a day or two, let us have some time off." He picked up the calendar on the counter, one of those cheap, plastic numbers with a daily aphorism written in cursive under the date. "'Tuesday,' read Taylor. "'Live every day like it's your last.' Think that's someone's idea of a joke?"

"Could be," said Murpam.

"Tell me more about him," said Taylor. The Subject hadn't ever visited the bookshop.

"Not much to tell," said Murpam. He opened the book to the first page, started to read.

"I hear he embezzled from the widows-and-orphans fund," said Taylor. "Got his sentence commuted when he became a Subject." Taylor packed his bag up. "You coming to the Boar and Barrister tonight?"

That night, after beers with Taylor, Murpam tore off the top sheet from the calendar, exposing Wednesday's date and quote, but the next morning it was Tuesday again.

Six weeks after Murpam lost track of days, The Subject came back into the store. Before Murpam could deliver his line The Subject leaned forward accusingly. "How much are light bulbs?" he asked. He wasn't a tall man, but broad in the shoulders. His face was hard and rough like a weather-beaten deck.

Light bulbs were the one item in the store that had a fixed price as far as Murpam was

Photograph by Jeff Winner

concerned. "Two ninety-nine," he said. The Subject fished out three dollar bills and pushed them across the counter to Murpam, who was glad he spent a couple of afternoons messing with the cash register. He slid a penny to The Subject, who snatched it up.

Murpam noticed The Subject had paid for light bulbs but wasn't actually carrying any. "You, uh, want help picking some out?" Murpam asked.

The Subject looked back at him. "No," he said, eyes unfocused. He ambled over and grabbed a pack off the shelf, then left.

Murpam was popular that night at the Boar and Barrister. Dozens of the bit actors had no interaction with The Subject at all, hardly caught a glimpse of him from across the street. Even Diller came over with her tonic and lime and sat at his table for a while, listening politely.

His tongue loosened by beer, Murpam recounted his first encounter several times over. "I had no idea," he said, "what light bulbs cost." Everyone laughed, even Diller.

"Were you scared?" she asked, leaning forward.

"Nope," said Murpam. Then he grinned. "Terrified."

The table laughed again, and Murpam leaned back. He put his hand on the back of Diller's chair, careful not to touch her, but she got up and disappeared. Someone bought another round, and Murpam told the story again for Taylor and a bearded man from Traffic, hoping Diller would return, but her chair remained empty until the bar closed.

He staggered down both blocks of Main Street, weaving from streetlight to streetlight. Just past the bank he leaned against a mailbox and peered at the half moon, pinned high and tiny in the clear night.

Outside the hardware store he found the dark, hulking van of Props and Replacements idling menacingly. He opened his door slowly, then stumbled over the threshold, knocking over a stand of postcards. Immediately several dim, red headlamps whipped around to face him, and quiet steps approached. He froze, terrified, as a dark figure picked up the postcard rack. Then two pairs of hands guided him through the aisles and upstairs to bed.

The next day The Subject was back, and again the day after that. Each time he paid for a pack of light bulbs, took his change and exited with mere scraps of conversation. Murpam's instructions never varied, and he delivered his opening line with what he considered reasonable aplomb.

After seven days of this, Taylor made his semiregular appearance with his backpack full of novels. "You're quite the talk of the town," he told Murpam. "You and The Subject appear to be bosom buds." He lifted himself on the counter and adopted a conspiratorial air. "I got a visit from Management. They asked me about you." He waggled his eyebrows, two dancing caterpillars over leering eyes.

Murpam tried to look calm. He knew Management visited the Leads — The Subject's roommate, neighbors, boss and coworkers — twice a week. Rumor was each of these visits included a personal chef and masseuse, and another attendant of a more intimate nature. Supposedly they made a thousand times what Murpam or Taylor or any of the other Bits made, and were on the fast track for television gigs once the shoot had run its course.

"One of 'em was a lady," said Taylor. He sighed. "She put a little 'h' sound in front of all of her 'w's," he said. "I think I'm in love."

"What did you tell them?" said Murpam.

Taylor looked up at the ceiling. "Hhh-what can you tell me about Mr. Murpam?" he quoted, dreamily. "Hhhwhen and hhhwhere did you first meet?"

The phone rang, startling them both. It had never rung before. Murpam didn't even know it was plugged in. He answered, "Hello?"

"New instructions have arrived from Management," said the telephone. The voice was tinny and stern. "You are to inform Subject you are out of light bulbs and have been for months."

"Out?" said Murpam.

"Subject is approaching. Arrival imminent."

Murpam hung up the phone and looked at Taylor. "I'm out of light bulbs," he said.

Taylor looked over at the shelves. "No, you're not," he said.

The bell above the door jingled, and in walked The Subject. He grabbed a two-pack of light bulbs.

Murpam blinked. "What can I do for you?" he said. Taylor jumped down off the counter.

"Light bulbs," said The Subject, sliding the two-pack across the countertop.

Murpam's eyes flickered to Taylor and then back to The Subject. "I'm out," he said.

"What?" said The Subject.

"I'm out," said Murpam.

"Out?"

"Of light bulbs," said Murpam, lamely. "Been out for months." He managed not to look down at the package on the countertop.

The Subject narrowed his eyes, then reached and grabbed Murpam's collar, dragging him forward across the counter until their noses almost touched. "I'm onto you," he whispered. "I'm not living the same day over and over. You assholes are messing with me."

Murpam's heels were off the ground, his stomach digging into the edge of the counter.

"You want to know how I know?" said The Subject. "How I know you're fucking with me?"

Murpam raised his eyebrows, hopefully sympathetically.

"The pennies," The Subject whispered. "I swallow them."

He didn't continue, and Murpam felt he should contribute. "Oh," he said.

The Subject relaxed his grip on Murpam's collar minutely. "The next day, I wake up. And everyone's telling me it's Tuesday again, saying the same goddam things they said yesterday."

"It is Tuesday," squeaked Taylor.

The Subject ignored him. "But I drink coffee, I drink prune juice. I eat a bran muffin. You know what comes out?"

Murpam knew but he didn't want to say. The grip on his collar tightened again and he gave in. "Pennies?"

"Pennies," said The Subject. He opened and closed his mouth. "Tell me," he said. "Tell me it's not Tuesday today."

Murpam swallowed, then lifted a sweaty hand and pointed to the calendar on the counter. "I don't know what to tell you," he said. "It's Tuesday." Then Murpam winked, slowly, his eye mere inches from The Subject's.

The tension sagged out of The Subject, who let go of Murpam's collar and smoothed down his shirtfront. "Tuesday," he said. "Right."

The next day, The Subject set fire to half the town, and the day after that Management called it a wrap.

Taylor's crush from Management interviewed Murpam in her office. "Hhhwhy," she said, "do you think The Subject decided to burn down the set? The day after talking to you?"

Murpam shrugged. "Probably the pennies," he said.

"Hmm," she said, and leaned back. She was a wisp of a woman, with wrists so thin Murpam imagined they were translucent. "You realize," she said, "that if hhhwe find proof you broke character, hhhwe don't have to pay you a single cent."

"If it was one of The Subject's pennies," said Murpam, "I'm not sure I would want it."

The cast had a wrap party at The Boar and Barrister, which survived the blaze. Wilson was back and spent most of the time arguing with his Russian counterpart about the nuances of his character, who, in Murpam's opinion, didn't do anything really other than wait for the bus.

The Subject entered to great applause and took a bow. He gave a little speech about his embezzlement conviction, about how the Producers and Researchers gave him another shot at life, however confusing and involuntary. He closed by apologizing for the fire with mock humility. Everyone laughed and applauded.

After his speech, The Subject wandered through the crowd making small talk and posing for pictures. Soon he wandered over to Murpam, who was four beers into the evening. "Light-bulb man!" he said, and gave Murpam a hug.

"Hiya," said Murpam. "How are you holding up?"

"Great," said The Subject. "The show's going to air in a couple of months, and part of the deal is my sentence got shortened. In three weeks I'm a free man."

Murpam nodded and looked out over the crowd at Taylor, who was chatting up Diller.

"Already got some talks lined up with insurance agencies, might be a spokesperson for some fire and arson policies."

"Not too shabby," said Murpam.

"Anyway," said The Subject, looking at Murpam out of the sides of his eyes. "Thanks for the light bulbs." He winked, grinning, and walked off.

Murpam finished his beer and tracked down Taylor, who had given up on Diller. "I hear they're hiring for a new show," said Taylor. "They're sending some poor sap back in time. We get to wear period costumes, talk funny, the whole enchilada." He raised his eyebrows. "I could put your name in, if you're interested," he said.

"Sure," said Murpam.

On the Train to Chicago

by

Alec Clayton

I was eighteen and thought I was a man. What eighteen-year-old doesn't? I had joined the Navy Reserve and was headed to Chicago for boot camp at Great Lakes Training Center on a train from New Orleans. Just a country boy from Podunk, Mississippi, I had never been on a train. I'd never even been out of Mississippi except for a couple of fishing trips with my old man, one to Louisiana and one to Florida.

I ordered pancakes for breakfast, not knowing if breakfast was included with the ticket — provided by good old Uncle Sam — or if I'd have to pay. I didn't want to ask for fear of seeming gauche. A surly waiter plopped down a plate with two pancakes on it — no butter, no syrup. I didn't want to ask for butter and syrup for the same reason I hadn't asked if breakfast was included in the ticket price. Maybe people who rode trains ate their pancakes dry. Maybe only country folk from Podunk poured syrup over them, so I choked them down as best I could.

To say I was not exactly worldly would be an understatement. I was a bumpkin — but not as much of a bumpkin as Randy, the sailor from Pelahatchie I met at the station. I don't think he'd ever been away from his daddy's peanut farm. He was tall and gangly with dry hair and buck teeth. I thought he looked like Li'l Abner. He sounded like he was shouting through a megaphone whenever he spoke.

Just to impress upon you how unsophisticated we were, let me jump ahead a moment to after boot camp, when they sent us to Washington, D.C. We did the usual tourist things — visited the Lincoln Memorial, walked around the mall, climbed all 897 steps of the Washington Monument and stared through the fence at the White House. I stared as much at the other tourists as I did at the big house.

Art by Scott Hammond

There were cowboys and Indians (both kinds of Indians), Blacks, whites and people with every imaginable kind of dress. "Look at all these people," I said to Randy, and that was when Randy, with a voice I was sure could be heard in Virginia, shouted out, "Gawldurnit" — yes, he really did say gawldurnit — "Gawldurnit, everybody up here wears shoes!"

I wanted to sink into the sidewalk.

That night we went to a bar where Randy picked up an older woman (probably every bit of twenty-eight). She invited him to come home with her and insisted I come along. At her apartment, we discovered she had a six-year-old daughter being babysat by a teenager. She paid the babysitter and the babysitter skedaddled. Randy and the woman went off into the bedroom to make whoopee while I kept the kid entertained. That's the kind of guy I was — the kind of guy who distracts the kid while my friend gets laid.

Back to the train trip to Chicago. We met a couple of other sailors heading to Great Lakes. They were from Memphis and clearly a lot more worldly than we were. They'd been to Chicago before, and one had even been to New York City. We played poker in the club car late into the night, drinking whisky and telling tales. They talked about all the women they had been with and told us they'd take us to a whorehouse they knew about in Chicago.

After four or five drinks, I had to go to the bathroom. I staggered my way forward in the rocking train, dizzy and disoriented from the booze and the movement of the train. I couldn't find the men's room and was getting desperate to pee. I went as far forward as I could possibly go, through car after car, then turned around and made my way back, holding myself by then and — I confess it — leaking a little in my dress white uniform. I swear to God, there were no bathrooms on that train.

Then I came up with a brilliant idea. There were sleeper cars with hammock-like bunks that sagged in the middle, and there were cars with regular seats. While trudging car-to-car, I noticed there were a lot of empty seats and people were sleeping in the few that were occupied. I figured I could pee in my hammock and then go sleep in one of the unoccupied seats. No problem.

So which bunk was mine? They all looked alike, but I remembered it was the second one in on the right — only, well, you know, I was drunk and disoriented and really didn't know if I was headed toward the engine or the caboose. I found what I thought was my bunk and unbuttoned the thirteen buttons of my sailor suit (buttons symbolizing the thirteen original colonies, we were told) and let loose.

That was when the woman screamed. "Help! Rape!" Within seconds three big train cops grabbed me and hustled me off to, of all places, the men's room. They slammed me against a wall and held me there and peppered me with questions. I tried my best to answer them as meekly as possible while holding my pants up with one hand and trying not to pee anymore. "No," I said. "I didn't touch the woman. I didn't even know she was there. I was … I was … I guess I was sleepwalking. I thought I was in the men's room. I just had to pee."

Finally, one of the cops left, came back and said, "I talked to the woman and she corroborates his story. He didn't touch her, he just peed on her. She said he must've been sleepwalking." She actually said sleepwalking, as if she had known that was my excuse and was covering for me.

The cops took my name and serial number and said they were going to report the incident to my commanding officer. I spent the whole two weeks of boot camp terrorized I was going to be tossed in the brig, maybe given a dishonorable discharge. I was horrified I would have to explain it to my mother back home, but I never heard another word about it.

I thought about it in that woman's apartment in Washington, D.C. One thing I did while I was there was open up her dictionary and look up the word "corroborate."

It Matters

by

Aidan Kelly

The Gnostics knew the All
is in the All and is a fullness.
My friend Kip Thorne has heard
The sound of collapsing stars
ripple through that fullness.
Perhaps stars converse by gravity,
but the angels, who fly,
take themselves lightly.

Wheeler knew electrons are
aware and know about each other.
Entangled, they never separate,
are perhaps as married,
however far apart,
as a woman praying
for the western wind to blow.
Perhaps that's how we know
what logic says is much too far away.

Art by Kristen Orlando

Electrons are pure energy.

If they're aware,

we know that matter,

if not conscious,

would not exist at all.

Since energy condenses

into matter, be aware

our brains do not

create our minds.

They condense

what's already there.

In their quirkiness, particles

are true or charmed or beautiful

in their eightfold way.

We tell two identical diamonds apart

by where they are, but particles

and angels are everywhere

until they're seen.

As Pauli and Aquinas knew,

were two of them the same,

they'd be just one, not two.

As everything that lives is holy,

All that's holy lives, and thinks.

Rocks think long, slow thoughts.

They have earthquakes

when they've had enough

of storing it all up.

The smell of fresh-cut grass
is the grass calling to the other grass
for help or as a warning.

Tree roots reach out to other roots,
feed their sap to fresh-cut stumps
to help them grow new shoots.

Sometimes that person called a cat,
especially one with seven toes,
having watched you turn
a faucet on, will try that too,
and flood the kitchen floor.

Electrons are not like marbles
nor protons like a bowling ball.
We would do as well to suppose,
since truth and beauty are all we know,
it's fairies dancing on their toes,
each by all, who by their play
Charm the angels to come and stay.

Babies see more colors than adults.
Toddlers are too young to know
they cannot see the fairies and angels
whom adults, unless gifted
by innocence, will never see again.

Die Einhornjäger

by

Justin Teerlinck

Art by Scott Hammond

October 18th, 1915

First World War

Eastern Europe

Dear Mum,

It ain't so bad up here. There's no sign of the enemy. Unicorn duty is as easy as they said it would be. We passed through a villa called Mort. There was a fountain in the village square. The town was deserted except for a funny old man who kept giggling and telling us the water would purify our souls and strengthen us as it had for centuries. All the boys drank and found it the cleanest and freshest since we left Cardiff. Lieutenant Thornton says we can get all the game we want, and Dell and Franks got two large hares. We haven't so much as touched the bully beef. I hope you and Dad have enough coal. I do miss your spotted dick and pork pies. Don't tell Sissy, but I got her a pipe or a whistle. I found it just before we got to town. It was lying in the dirt by a berry patch, hanging from a bush, most strange. Almost like someone left it there to be found. It makes a funny humming noise. Let's us say it's from Father Christmas, hey?

Your ever loving son,

Private Danvers

B Company

51st Regiment, Her Majesty's Anti-Unicorn Brigade

My darling wife,

The men are exceedingly idle. They treat the campaign as one big lark. I suppose it is. Several German unicorn divisions are known to be operating in our sector. They call us Die Einhornjäger, the unicorn hunters. They call themselves the Einhornwaffe. We've never actually seen any. Well, no one has since The Awfully Unfortunate Incident. It is said that in spite of this, they greatly fear us. The spiraled-horned monsters are no match for our Vickers guns and gas bombs. The Vickers can fire 500 rounds a minute to well over a mile. The Enfield rifles fire rounds at over 2,000 feet per second. We even have a support tank and several men carry elephant guns "just in case." Our mission, at present, is to find the men of the 231st Anti-Unicorn Brigade, meet up with them and engage the enemy. The boys are itching for a fight. We want to show queen and country that we are made of stern stuff! We likely haven't found our brothers in arms because they are operating behind enemy lines, or at least that is what Field Marshal Lansford says. The men are confident in his command. He has a scar across his face and wears an eyepatch, having lost an eye in a skirmish with our mythical quarry. He is the only man in the field with firsthand experience with these homicidal beasts.

Lieutenant Thornton
Commanding Officer
B Company
51st Regiment, Her Majesty's Anti-Unicorn Brigade

October 28th, 1915

Auxiliary Supply Corps

Our lines are stretched thin, making regular communication difficult. The requisitions for fresh meat, rum, biscuits, fuel for the tanks, and machine-gun ammunition have not been fulfilled. Field Marshal Lansford wishes to know if they have been received and if so, what the delay is. As we penetrate deeper into wild country in an expeditionary capacity, it is all the more necessary that we are adequately supplied. The boys will be quite disappointed if they run out of Duffy's Tip Top Pipe Powder (the finest pipe powder that ever peeped from a pipe) and don't get any lamb shank for Guy Fawkes Day. Please advise on feasibility of request.

Ian Withers

Supply Officer

51st Regiment, Her Majesty's Anti-Unicorn Brigade

Guy Fawkes Day, 1915

Classified Sensitive Communiqué

Intelligence Division

Need to Know Only

We entered the hamlet of Verboten in want of fresh meat and other provisions. At first the senior officers were able to control the junior officers who controlled the noncommissioned officers who controlled the men who controlled the horses who controlled the oats and hay. The men all began acting strangely upon drinking from the village well. Rum rations have dwindled to nary a thimbleful per day, and the undisciplined rogues imbibed our entire store of Mrs Right Away's Tincture of Opium Cure All. In the village we found elderly civilians and young girls. They all had a way about them, smiling, unconcerned with our presence. The men and officers did not like their attitude. We found pagan relics and a maypole, along with animal sacrifices. "Where are the fighting men?" the translator asked. "Fighting," was the reply. "And where are the Einhornwaffe?" To this, the village folk laughed at us and said we had been reading too many Greek legends. The interrogating officer showed the old man our badge and insignia, and yelled that our queen thought it was serious enough to warrant fighting about. The old man then grievously insulted Her Majesty — or so he thought. The translator's German wasn't terribly good. The officer then removed his glove and slapped the old man. A spirited girl near him said that was no way to treat her granddad, and so she slapped the interrogating officer, who then slapped her back and was in turn slapped by the old man.

The officers and men alike began to swoon and stagger and behave as drunkards. I was waxing my mustache at this time and therefore was unable to restore order. Looking in the mirror, I saw I had three eyes and five arms. The officers informed the village folk that slapping an officer in wartime was a hanging offence but, as this was deemed a formality, the officer merely drew his service revolver and shot them both where they stood. It is, of course, rather regrettable that unarmed civilians should be dispatched in this manner, especially when ammunition is at a premium. It is unclear who torched the first structure, or when the indiscriminate shooting began. Several unicorns were found hidden in barns, disguised as mortal horses. But when questioned, the horses admitted they were indeed unicorns. Their horns were disguised as farm implements hanging in the barn. They refused to reveal the location of their secret camp, so they were shot, butchered and eaten. This was allowed as a wartime liberty, but when the men sought relations with the young maidens, I mounted my steed and rode about the village commanding a cessation of all mischief. The next day I awoke with the right half of my mustache gone. Even under penalty of death the men and officers to a man swore an oath I did not shout a single order but merely rode about the village with my saber drawn, clucking like a chicken. All the civilians, living and dead, had disappeared. Our propaganda officer tacked a note to the front door of the town hall. It read thus:

Good people of the town of Verboten, we were within the law to make execute/shooting of the bad old mister and many girls who make a bad word on our Queen (who is Best). Still, we regret burning of this, all your houses, and so much the killing. We find this quite unfortunate. We are not Mr. Dumbhead. We know you unicorn feed and make a pony house! Give it up! We find. We kill. However, just give us the unicorn and make friends, give you ale, and have bawdy dances with beer barrels and singing "one, two, down the hatch." Okay? Goodbye beautifully.

Your British Best Friends Forever … Maybe (you pick)?

Field Marshal Lansford (The Man With Shiniest Hat)

51st Regiment, Her Majesty's Anti-Unicorn Brigade

November 16th, 1915

Dearest Father,

The men grow thin and even more wan and pasty than dictated by our climate and heritage. An advance squad found them and had the good sense to discreetly inform me so as not to arouse a general panic. I investigated with Captain Ellison of C Company and Captain Harris of D Company. What we found must never be spoken of before the boys. The bodies were unmistakably ours; the corpses were naked and mutilated, arranged in a pentagram, but their uniforms were found folded neatly nearby without a single tear or a drop of blood on them. They all bore the insignia of the 231st. They were all officers, just a handful. On one of the bodies was found written in blood: "We slake our thirst on the blood of the unicorn hunters." That was all. After they were buried, stout-hearted men were selected by their officers to scour the nearby woods in hope of finding the others, while the remainder dug entrenchments and made defensive fortifications. No other souls were ever found. There was more, much more I saw that I shall never forget, but it was too shocking to put to paper. May God walk with us always. Ask the vicar to keep us in his daily prayers. Burn this letter after you read it, and never let Mum or Martha see it. I am,

Your ever loving son,

Lieutenant Thornton

Commanding Officer

B Company

51st Regiment, Her Majesty's Anti-Unicorn Brigade

November 21st, 1915

Dear Mum,

The boys hate to admit it, but they are right terrified. The night watches swear they see red eyes and spiraled horns at the edge of the wood. I blow my strange whistle for the comforting melodies it imparts. Several false alarms resulted in the expenditure of much ammunition, which incensed the officers to no small degree. All we have to eat is Mrs Right Away's Stool Softening Digestive Biscuit. That along with the prune juice causes the men to need the latrine. Some have taken to using their helmets or the trenches to answer this need, out of fear of the woods. Much of the bully beef was green. But even with our innards turning to jelly, it's stiff upper lip and a brave face for whatever unseen menace awaits us in the dark. Tell Sissy I love her and give Father a manly handshake from me.

Private Danvers

B Company

51st Regiment, Her Majesty's Anti-Unicorn Brigade

p.s. Could you please send a tin of Mrs Right Away's Emergency Reusable Toilet Tissue?

November 30th, 1915

My dearest darling wifey poo,

All is well. They struck at dawn, hitting our strongest defenses. It was snowing heavily midst the pine woods. Forty war 'corns sallied boldly at our best entrenched position in a suicidal frontal assault. Some were riderless. Others were mounted by Jerries wearing nothing but a loincloth and German army helmets, wielding small arms and primitive stabbing weapons such as swords and pikes. The men formed ranks and hit them with volley fire. The Vickers-gun crewmen acquitted themselves admirably, cutting down an advance squad of hostiles before they reached our lines. The tanks took to the field but were too slow and cumbersome, and easily outmaneuvered like great, fire-spitting tortoises. It didn't matter. In ten minutes of firing we routed the attack and gave spirited pursuit, cutting down the retreating stragglers. None were taken alive. On our side only a few were wounded, and fewer yet lost — most to gorings of the poisonous horn. Only a few of the fleetest Einhornwaffe made it out, breaking for the black mountains in the distance. Morale is higher than it's been in weeks. It's as if the horrors and strange things we've seen had never transpired. Keep us in your prayers. Tomorrow we give further chase after the spiraled menace.

    Lieutenant Thornton

    Commanding Officer

    B Company

    51st Regiment, Her Majesty's Anti-Unicorn Brigade

December 3rd, 1915

Classified Sensitive Communiqué

Intelligence Division

Need to Know Only

Advance force lost in mountain ambush. Do please send immediate reinforcements, if you would be so kind. Ninety percent attrition rate. Brigade surrounded. Ammunition is nearly depleted. It has been snowing for the past several days. The men are caught out in the open, freezing to death. A single horse and rider were sent south with the hopeless prayer that they will reach Central Command with these despatches. The enemy brooks no mercy. Attempts to surrender were met with the slaughter of unarmed men under flag of truce. They are savages. The men fought hand to hand, forming ranks. There was no time to make entrenchments in our current position. The horned devils found a method of disabling our tank treads, making further retreat impossible. They come at night. We see their eyes glowing red through the snow. Several enlisted men were sent into the forest to gather firewood. They never returned. A few officers have taken refuge inside the tanks with limited food and water. During one of the night raids, a unicorn horn burst through the three-inch-thick steel tank armor and pierced Major William's liver. He died the next day, delirious with fever, raving and begging for one last pipe of Duffy's Pipe Powder. We lit it and held it to his lips, but they turned blue and he expired before taking a single puff. The terrors they inflict on us are unspeakable. We shall use the last stores of petrol to make torches to warm and defend ourselves when the ammunition is gone. We can hold out for perhaps two days, perhaps less. Honestly, it isn't so bad. The men bear their trials with steely resolve and stoic manliness. Stiff upper lip and once more unto the breach, as they say. Where once we feared the barbed-wire fences and virgin guards of a unicorn prison-labour camp, we now make ready to meet an honorable death in the field. God save the queen. God save us from the Einhornwaffe.

Field Marshal Lansford

Supreme Commander

51st Regiment, Her Majesty's Anti-Unicorn Brigade

The Disappeared

by

Jonny Eberle

It was dusk when Esteban left. The shutters had been closed for six days and the apartment reeked of candle smoke and wine. His mother refused to allow any light in until Esteban's brother's body was found and he was starting to fear that the shutters would stay closed forever. There would never be a body to bury. There never was. Esteban couldn't stand it anymore — mourning and waiting for news that would never come.

So he took his brother's rusty yellow bicycle from under the stairs and went out. The spring air was cool on his face. Fresh air rushed down the wooded hillsides into the city, clearing the smog temporarily. Esteban wasn't allowed outside after sunset, not since Oscar Pérez's disappearance.

Esteban was hiding in the alley, drinking a warm beer he'd stolen from his brother, when a van pulled up to the house across the street. Three men came out and broke down the door. A few minutes later, the men carried Pérez out of the house with a bag over his head, tossed him into the back of the van and drove off. Esteban told his mother about the abduction. He didn't tell her why he had been outside but suspected she could smell the beer on his breath.

On those cold winter nights, Esteban's brother went to the cemetery after dinner to smoke stale cigars with his friends. Their mother would drink a glass of wine and tell Esteban stories of her childhood on her family's banana plantation, how they were forced off their land and came to the city for work. How she was planning to save enough to buy a house by the sea where she could plant a banana grove and teach her sons to love the soil.

"Miguel, do you think Pérez was a communist?" Esteban asked his brother one afternoon. They were on their way home from the market. Esteban was walking in the shade of the tall apartment buildings. His brother balanced a sack of rice on the handlebars of the bicycle.

"Where did you hear that?"

"The girls in the apartment downstairs," Esteban said. "They said he was a union leader and he had a secret family in the mountains."

"You know they like to tease you, Esteban," Miguel said. "I wouldn't listen to them."

"Why did they take him, then?"

"You want to know what I think?" They crossed the street. Sirens wailed on the breeze. Miguel checked to make sure no one was following them before he spoke. "They took him because he's a smart man, and smart men do not stand by when terrible things happen — They ask questions."

"What kind of questions?" Esteban asked.

"You're a smart man, too, little brother. That can be dangerous."

Esteban held the rice while Miguel chained his bicycle to the staircase. Inside, the apartment was filled with the smell of black beans boiling. Their mother was in the kitchen, cooking and listening to the radio. Thirty people were dead at the Spanish embassy. The general was on the radio railing against the terrorists who burned themselves alive along with

Art by Jenni Prange Boran

their hostages. He vowed to destroy the enemies of the people. Esteban lay awake that night, unable to sleep as he listened to the sirens echoing through the city.

Gravity was pulling the bicycle now and Esteban stood on the pedals to coast down the hill. Up ahead, the cars were backed up, waiting to get through an intersection congested with evening traffic. The exhaust was warm on his legs as he wove between the stopped cars.

Two cars had bumped fenders and the owners were standing in the street, yelling about who would pay for the damage. An army truck idled in the intersection, waiting for the drivers to clear the road. A row of young men stood in the back of the truck with rifles slung over their shoulders — One looked like an old school friend. Esteban slowed to a stop. A soldier climbed down from the truck and walked over to the men arguing on the street. His hand was on his pistol.

Esteban didn't wait to see what happened next. He turned down an alley to his left and pedaled hard. The bicycle was heavy underneath him, so he stood up to drive the pedals with the weight of his body. The rattle of the bicycle chain reverberating off the high walls was deafening. Partway down the alley, the walls were plastered with black-and-white photos: men and women of all ages who watched him as he pedaled by. Below each photo were a name and date.

Two weeks earlier, Esteban walked in on his brother in the bathroom with a bloody washcloth in his hand. "What the hell is this?"

"I had a disagreement with a man at the market, that's all," Miguel said. "Get out of here and close the door." Esteban stepped into the bathroom and shut the door. Miguel was bleeding badly from a cut behind his right ear.

"You'll never stop it that way," Esteban said. He took the washcloth from Miguel and pressed it hard against the cut. "Hold it there." Esteban rummaged in the cupboard for the rubbing alcohol.

"Do you remember Antonio Ruiz? He used to work for the newspaper," Miguel said. "He disappeared on his way to work three days ago. There's a rumor he got picked up, so a few friends organized a demonstration at the market."

"I take it that it wasn't peaceful." Esteban found the bottle and dabbed the tip of a clean towel into the rubbing alcohol.

"It was peaceful until one of the soldiers on patrol started throwing rocks at us."

Esteban shot him an incredulous look.

"Okay, we started throwing rocks. But I wasn't trying to hit any of them. Then one came at me and beat me with the butt of his rifle."

Esteban took the bloody washcloth from Miguel and started to clean the cut. Miguel flinched.

"Hold still," Esteban said. "Father Guillermo said today that we aren't supposed to fight back, you know. We're supposed to turn the other cheek."

"Father Guillermo is an idiot. I can't sit by while people are attacked in their homes and whole villages are being butchered."

"You could've been shot. That doesn't get Antonio Ruiz back, or Oscar Pérez, or anyone."

"It isn't about one man, little brother," Miguel said. "People disappear every day and we don't talk about it. I can't take it anymore and I don't care what Father Guillermo says."

"Fine," Esteban said. "Go to your demonstrations, but be careful." Miguel placed the cloth in the sink and put his hands on his brother's shoulders.

"What I do, I do for you," Miguel said. "Remember that when they come for me."

Esteban emerged from the alley into the marketplace. On either side of the road, booths sprang up like grass through sidewalk cracks. Merchants clamored for attention, selling beans, flour, chicken and Holy Week lilies. Esteban rode through the crowd, dodging women who balanced baskets on their heads.

Esteban wondered if his brother walked this way. A few hours before his disappearance, Esteban found his brother on the roof with an American he'd never seen before. They were drinking, laughing and eating greasy pupusas.

"Miguel, it's time for dinner," Esteban called to him. Miguel didn't seem to hear, so Esteban climbed over the loose tiles and cupped his hands around his mouth. "Miguel!" Miguel and his new friend turned around.

"I'm not hungry," Miguel said through a mouthful of food.

"Who is this man?" Esteban clenched his fists.

"It's okay, little brother. He's here to fight with us."

"What does he know about our fight?" Esteban stormed off without giving his brother a chance to answer. That was the last time he saw him. Not long after, Miguel left with his friend for a dissidents' meeting, was stopped by armed men on the side of the road, was beaten and dragged into the back of a truck. That was the end of it. There would be no acknowledgement of his death, no notice in the paper, no funeral, no grave. No one died anymore. They simply vanished and were forgotten.

Esteban dreamt that night that his brother had somehow escaped and was fighting with the rebels in the mountains. Instead of rotting in an unmarked grave by the side of the road, he was leading the charge to liberate their grandfather's banana grove. He saw his brother's face on wanted posters that called him an enemy of the people, instead of plastered on walls that listed the names of the missing.

He could barely see where he was going through the tears welling in his eyes as he rode into the plaza. He pedaled harder. Instead of braking as he approached the church, he drove the pedals with all the strength he could summon to his aid. The bicycle rattled up the stone steps, nearly shaking the screws out of the frame. Esteban rode up the steps of the church and through the open door, then let the bicycle coast. The clink of gears and the squeak of wheels echoed in the rafters.

It was four days before Palm Sunday and the church was empty except for the parade floats being readied for the festivities of Holy Week. On Sunday, they would be carried through streets carpeted with flower petals, but now they sat unfinished in the aisles. He coasted past scenes of Judas' betrayal and Peter's denial before coming to a stop before a wooden replica of Jesus crowned with thorns and crawling under the lash of Roman guards. Esteban let the bicycle fall to the ground.

Father Guillermo rushed out of the sacristy to see what the commotion was about. He was still in his black shirt and white collar after leading evening prayers and hearing confessions.

"Esteban, what are you doing here? Is someone following you?"

"No, Father. I don't think so."

Father Guillermo looked back the way Esteban had come, checking for armed men at the door.

"You should not be out at night," the priest said. "It's not safe. Not even here."

"I don't care," Esteban said. "They can kill me if they like."

"You're angry. You have a right to be," Father Guillermo said. He laid a hand on Esteban's shoulder. "I'm sorry about your brother."

"I don't understand why they took him, Father."

"We may never understand."

"He was dangerous. He asked too many questions. Maybe that's why."

"This is a dangerous time to be alive," Father Guillermo said. "Maybe they were coming after him, or maybe he was simply at the wrong place at the wrong time. There may not be any reason for it."

"God did this. He let this happen."

"Men did this. But God feels our pain. He weeps with us."

"That isn't enough."

"No, I suppose that isn't much comfort," Father Guillermo said. "But it's the only sermon I have to offer."

Esteban looked at the figure of the crawling Christ on the float, his face twisted in anguish and eyes pleading heavenward. The fresh paint glistened in the candlelight. Esteban reached out to touch it and let his hand slide over the carved surface. The eyes and face smeared into a blur.

Father Guillermo walked him home through the twisting, darkened streets. Esteban's mother pinched his ear for disobeying her and making her worry. Father Guillermo offered his condolences and said a blessing before leaving.

"Go to bed," his mother said after she closed the door. Her hands were shaking and the skin around her eyes shimmered with tears. "Now."

Esteban went into the bedroom and pushed open the shutter. In the alley behind their apartment, two soldiers were smoking. A woman was leaning out of a window in the next building to hang her laundry to dry. Somewhere in the city, men and women were being dragged out of their beds. Far away, high in the mountains, men were fighting and dying in the mist. Esteban saw the war everywhere. He saw it in the curling smoke that rose from the end of a cigarette. He saw it in the flapping blouses pinned to the line, straining under the weight of wet cloth. He saw it in his mother's eyes when she entered the room. She sat next to him on the bed and wrapped her arms around him.

"I thought you were dead," she said.

"I'm sorry, mama," he said.

"You have to promise me you'll never go out like that again. I can't stand the thought of losing you both."

"I can't promise that," he said.

"But what if you disappear?" she asked.

"I think I already have."

God's Mailroom

by

Sean Michael Galvin

My dad drove us to the church

He unlocked the sanctuary door

And we followed him to the altar

He kneeled on the steps and began to pray

My brother followed suit

Like he knew what he was doing

With a half-open eye

I watched them

Hoping they wouldn't notice

I felt like I was cheating on a test

I interlocked my fingers

And closed my eyes tight

I tried to get there

Wherever they were

Or wherever they thought they were

Or wherever they were pretending to be

I tried to feel

Something

Anything

It was as if I were continually dialing the wrong number

"If you'd like to make a call, please hang up and try again."

It's not like I was one digit off

But more like I had the wrong area code altogether

My thoughts scattered

Like birds at the sound of a rifle

As my father's trembling voice echoed

In the empty sanctuary

I began to sweat

Where the fuck are You?

I'd always just gone through the motions

"Now I lay me down to sleep," blah blah blah

Lying in my bed at night, just sort of talking to the ceiling

Hoping some of the sentiments might rise and escape

Through the pegboard holes in the ceiling tiles

Travel through the attic and the roof

And maybe catch a ride on the belt loop of an ascending soul

On their way to heaven

Where they'd be tossed into a bin

In God's mailroom

Stacks upon stacks of prayers

Billions of them

To be sorted by the interns

And maybe

Someday

Make their way to his desk

Carved from stone

Polished by trespassers

Shiny as a taxman's head

Where He sits

In a camping chair

Puffing on a Pall Mall

A massive man

Shirtless

With a Florida tan

Maybe three to four percent body fat

Hair tied up in a man bun

Beachy waves and natural amber highlights

Dark-brown eyes

Like an oil spill

Long, ducktail eyelashes

A lengthy, well-groomed beard

Thick as an eagle's nest

Burly fingers

Covered in yellow calluses

From aggressively plucking at harp strings

Quads like a sequoia

Veins like garden hoses

Pumping the purest blood

Through His perfect vessel

High-octane

Additive-free

Oxygen-rich

Blood

Immune to the ills of earth

His feet kicked up on the desk

Size 19 Birkenstocks

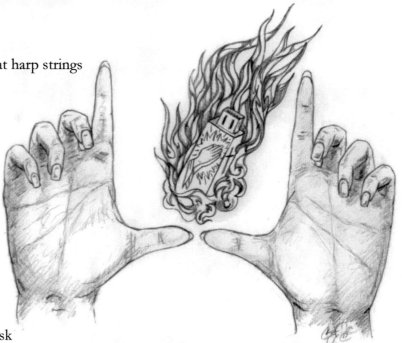

Art by Carrie Foster

A tight-bodied coed in nothing but a fig leaf

Struts over and sets a flash drive on His desk

"Here's the latest, Mr. Christ"

"Make a goal post, Janine."

He flicks it through the uprights

Leaving a trail of fire in its wake

"It's good!"

He picks up His iPhone and scrolls through the latest news

 He grabs a handful of Janine's ass and pulls her close

"Check this out, you gotta see this … It's hilarious."

They watch a live feed of my attempts at prayer and have a

good laugh

"Ah, good stuff … Good stuff."

"I'm tired. Go make me a Red Bull and vodka, Janine," says the

Lord.

Rosie's Café

by

Cathy Warner

The sign read Rosie's Café: Pets Welcome, People Tolerated. If Rosie had her way it would be only German shepherds and schnauzers that she served, but they didn't pay the bills, lacking opposable thumbs and pockets for wallets. Still, she imagined she could work out a system — sew small fabric pouches that fastened to collars that the owners could slip bills inside. Of course they'd have to prepay; she wouldn't trust an honor system, being reimbursed for biscuits and gravy.

So really, her sign ought to read Pets Welcome, People BARELY Tolerated, so when the campers wandered out of their tents and RVs in the mornings groggy-throated and bleary-eyed and shuffled to the camp store where Rosie's Café stood, they wouldn't expect a friendly greeting and inquiries about where they hailed from and where they were headed next.

Her café was nothing more than a lean-to next to a small Quonset hut that sold firewood, lighters, graham crackers, marshmallows and Jiffy Pop. Rosie kept a metal mixing bowl for the dogs next to the water spigot, and a glass jar filled with Milk Bone biscuits on her order counter. One free with purchase, her hand-lettered sign read, and she'd been in more than one argument with a dog owner who insisted that each item, a bagel, hash browns, eggs, counted as a separate purchase, and he — it was always a he who insisted — would reach for three Milk Bones. Whereas Rosie insisted a purchase was signified by the total she punched into her cash register, no matter how many items constituted that purchase.

She would hold out her hand until the greedy owner, unglued by her one-eyed glare, surrendered the extra Milk Bones. If the man had a wife or a girlfriend, she'd be the one to show up the next morning for breakfast, retriever slapping its tail against her legs.

It was amazing how many people camping at the lake, when given a choice, elected not to cook on their Coleman stoves — making the lure of hot, morning coffee even stronger than their repulsion of the ornery Rosie.

It wasn't simply her missing eye or her rationing of Milk Bones (she paid for them out of her own pocket, after all), or her apron emblazoned with the words Bite Me. It was something she gave off like an odor. Customers stood tense and stiff after placing their orders. No sitting at the picnic table chatting, laughing, having fun as if they were on vacation, which of course they were. The campers smoked when they were around Rosie, long, furious drags on Marlboros and Camels as if that might calm them. The nonsmokers chewed gum. The non-gum-chewers picked at their fingernails.

But the dogs, they liked her — loved her. They wandered away from their owners or tugged on leashes toward the screened door of Rosie's shack, where they lowered their haunches into the pine duff and cocked their heads toward the sounds of clattering pans, sizzling bacon and Rosie stomping in the tiny room. They whined high and long as if remembering they were wild once, and their ears twitched as if the spatula slapping the grill was the sound of prey and they were just biding time before making a kill. Rosie would hear the plaintive whines and nod imperceptibly in agreement, remembering her hunting days when she, Paul and her retriever, Jemma, sat in the duck blind on the far side of the lake waiting for the hard rustle and beat of wings as the geese rose off the water. She remembered the recoil of the rifle against her shoulder, the bruise it left in the soft flesh next to her collarbone. Back then she had her dog, a husband, both eyes and enough bird in the freezer to last through the winter.

Back then, things were different, and now … Well, now the dogs whined and Rosie growled. Every now and then she'd look up from her order pad — it was a voice with a certain timbre that made her lift her gaze to search the face — not that she believed in reincarnation, that her husband was inhabiting someone else's body, but she believed there was a set number of voices in the world and when one came close to Paul's she'd stop and consider its bearer — wonder for an instant if the voice belonged to a human to whom she might tell the truth. So far it hadn't happened.

It's not that her story was waiting to pour out of her into the ears of her dead husband's sound-alike, it was just that she felt her throat growing rusty from minimal use: "Can I take your order?" and "Give back them Milk Bones" and "Order's ready" lacked the sheer number and variety of syllables that had peppered her speech back when she squatted with Paul in the duck blind whispering about windchill factors and pin feathers, the new recipes she was itching to try and the down quilt she was steadily stuffing after each kill.

"I can't get in a word edgewise," Paul told her. It was true then and truer once the chew gnawed at his vocal cords, and later went his voice, surgically removed to keep the cancer from doing him in but it got him anyway.

Rosie'd gone to the duck blind that fall, just her and Jemma, and some dumbass discharged his rifle in the parking lot. The bullet ricocheted off his fender and hit Jemma clean through the heart. The shooter was drunk and bawling as he stood over Rosie, wringing his hands uselessly while she staunched the blood with her jacket, trying to get the jerk to help lift 73-pound Jemma into the car. But all he did was babble. Rage and grief knocked Rosie senseless then. She grabbed a branch sharpened and charred on one end — probably a campfire poker — and charged point-first into his chest letting out an unearthly howl. She succeeded in puncturing a full can of beer that was tucked in an inside pocket of his hunting vest. It hissed and leaked, and he staggered back looking as if he were pissing yellow from the belly.

She lunged for him. He rolled out from under her as they fell to the ground and somehow, the branch she brandished turned her blind fury perversely back to her own self, impaling her eye, some godawful, cartoonish injustice. The drunk jumped inside his Cherokee. She heard the doors lock and his voice frantic and loud, even through the rolled-up windows: "There's been an accident. It's an emergency." Then he started the engine and sped off, gravel spitting from under his tires, while she crawled on the ground toward Jemma.

Rosie dismissed the overtures of the hospital social worker who suggested therapy, saying she might have PTSD as if she were some Iraqi war vet. The social worker, all sympathetic smiles, left her card, phoned once a month, even came to the café once. And of course, Rosie hadn't actually told her the truth; same went for the police who stood by her bed asking questions while morphine stung her veins. In Rosie's story, it was an unfortunate shoot and run, the man accidently shooting his gun and her tripping on the upturned fire-ring poker as she ran for her dog. She didn't say he reeked of alcohol, didn't say she'd run at him first. In her recounting, it had all been an accident, improbable and bloody but free from aggravated assault.

She was lucky, the surgeon said, the branch hadn't punctured through to the brain. There was some internal bleeding, that was to be expected, but it would stop soon and she'd be fine. It would take some adjusting, of course — She could kiss her peripheral vision goodbye but could compensate easily enough by turning her head. He sent an occupational therapist to her room who gave her exercises to restore her depth perception in the form of pouring water from a plastic pitcher into a plastic cup, and by the time her bandages came off, the week after her discharge, Rosie could crack an egg on the side of a bowl with one hard blow just as she had before.

The café had been Paul's idea, along with moving to the lake when it became clear they weren't going to be, in his words, "blessed by the good Lord with offspring" and therefore had no need for living in town near schools and the library, ball fields and ballet studios. Paul found them a trailer and jobs as camp host and caretaker. Soon after they moved in, he started eyeing the shack next to the camp store. He signed a year's lease, sold some valuable Confederate coins, bought restaurant equipment, and soon Rosie's Café was a bona fide business.

Rosie was friendly enough when Paul was alive, even when he'd been rendered mute, even after she buried him at the little Free Methodist churchyard cemetery on the far side of the lake. But after Jemma died she became surly and snake-tempered. The worst part of that day hadn't been that she'd felt glee, the pure adrenaline rush of predator pleasure when she attacked the drunk hunter; it was that she hadn't been able to bury Jemma. Animal control disposed of Jemma's body — cremating her along with a passel of euthanized shelter dogs — while Rosie was laid up at County General. At the news, she blinked back tears in her good eye and wondered what was happening behind the gauze patch on the other. Had it gone dry, waterless and burned barren like the ground?

It'd been a drought year and Paul's death came on the heels of a forest fire that licked one side of the lake, choking out campers and wildlife, which is how she found herself hunting that day in a ravine the flames missed. The pines were flocked in ash, the ground smelled burnt and the temperatures refused to drop, but she would've clawed out a grave for Jemma there in a small clearing just off the trail in the lee of boulders where she and Jemma had crouched to eat breakfasts of cold bacon and biscuits.

Not my cub. Not my girl. Not my Jemma. That refrain still played in her sleep, waking her in a sweat nearly every night.

She thought it was her own lament, her own loud howling that woke her one night a year and a half after the tragedy, but as her own heart thudded wildly in her chest, she heard the howl again, tiny and high-pitched. She opened her eyes to find the full moon shining through the pop vent and sat up at the sound of a thin scratching on the trailer door.

The dog, mangy, muddy and matted, looked more like a rat or possum — it was just that size — and Jesus, it stank. Collarless and shaking, it darted in as soon as she cracked the door and hid under the banquette, its hairless tail quivering. She crouched to see the scrawny pup, shadowed in the dark. It whimpered under the table, and all she had in her refrigerator was months-old margarine and ketchup. She didn't keep Milk Bones in her trailer, and she'd stopped cooking for herself there as well. She ate at

Art by Carrie Foster

the café, scrambling an egg or grilling a burger alongside a customer order, even through the winter with the café closed. There was nothing for it but to pick up the dog and head for the café where she had some cooked bacon in the fridge.

"Here, pup," she said. "It's gonna be okay, pup." She slid her hand along the floor, palm up, fingers extended toward the shaking dog. She heard it sniff, felt its warm quick breath against her fingers and then the dog's wet tongue softly grazing her palm.

"Good pup." Rosie raised her hand and stroked the dog's wet back. Lord, was it bony. She cupped the pup's haunches and pulled the dog gently across the galley floor. The dog came willingly and when Rosie had it in full view, she scooped it to her chest and stood up. The dog couldn't have weighed more than a twin-pack of bread. A flea jumped onto Rosie's arm. She slapped at it.

Then she held the dog at arm's length for just a second to confirm its sex. "Well, that's a good girl," she said, feeling the wet of the dog's fur soaking into her T-shirt. The dog nuzzled Rosie's armpit. She was a terrier of some sort, small enough to fit easily into the sink at the café where Rosie could wash her with the spray hose. Rosie walked to the bathroom and pulled her bath towel off the rack, wrapped it around the shivering dog and rummaged a clean towel from the shelf above the toilet. She began formulating a plan, speaking aloud to the dog, her rusty voice loosening a little. "Bacon first, then a bath and when we get back here, I might still have a flea comb somewhere and we'll have you right as rain in no time. I just need my flashlight and the café key." Rosie lifted them off a hook near the door and slipped them into the pocket of her jacket hanging there. "And my jacket, if I can put you down for just a sec."

Rosie set the bundled pup on the table and shrugged on her jacket. The dog looked up at her, brown eyes shining though her lashes were caked with mud.

"I'd like to call you Pauli, if you don't mind," Rosie said as she picked up the pup again.

Pauli lifted her face and licked Rosie's cheek.

Boggy
by
Jonah Barrett

I cannot tell what are dreams and what are memories anymore, and I hope this will not hurt me. I can recall running through grass with my brother, blackberry cobbler in the kitchen, and catching white moths in jars. But I also remember calls in the night, shapes in the water and a set of cold eyes. I think back on laughing, screaming, nettle stings, sweetness and a sense of eternal summer, everlasting youth. I rarely recaptured that last feeling later in life, but when I did it was with my friend Jill.

The two of us set up the tent in the middle of the bog, where the grass was a dry yellow and the dirt was practically sand. She didn't want to pitch it too close to the water, because she said she didn't want one of us rolling out in the middle of the night and drowning in our sleep, but I think there was another reason. I think Jill was scared, and rightly so. There was something wrong about that water: a murky black that seemed much deeper than the ten feet my brother had told me. I couldn't look at it for too long; neither could Jill. It was like avoiding eye contact. I know that's ridiculous. I knew the water in bogs weren't able to sustain life. And yet …

I told Jill we didn't have to pitch the tent so early; it was only 3:00. She said she wanted to establish a home base early on.

We need somewhere familiar to return to after each of our numerous exploits!" she said in that deep faux-superhero voice she used all the time. I loved that voice. It was playful and bold all at once, and made the mundane reality of life almost seem bearable.

"D'ya think we should set an alarm system?" she asked, a rascal grin electrifying her face.

I laughed. "Whaddya mean?"

"You know, twine, clanging cans, that sorta stuff. I've always wanted to do it," she said. Jill always felt as if she'd jumped straight from the pages of a Mark Twain novel. I wouldn't have been surprised if I had caught her training frogs, and an alarm system didn't catch me off guard, either.

"Why would we need an alarm system?" I asked.

She shrugged, wistfully looking up at the sky like she had a secret. "I dunno. Animals? Forest men? Take your pick. We're stranded in the wilderness, Anita. Anything could happen."

She winked at me, and I swallowed my feelings. That last part about the wilderness was a bit of a fib, playful make-believe we both know wasn't true. Home base sat in the center of a mini-peninsula, surrounded by bog water. Behind us loomed a large hill covered in pines with my family's house located just beyond that. We were less than half a mile away from the comfort of Netflix marathons and roofs, but Jill wanted to make a spectacle of this. She was leaving for college in a few days. This was to be our last official "slumber party," a final farewell to the title before it devolved into just "hanging out" and then later "catching up." Jill loved slumber parties growing up, and she also loved camping. I came up with the idea of combining the two. My parents didn't know we were here, either.

I held up a bucket by the handle — one of two we brought.

"Tonight, okay?" I said.

She smiled, sighing, and took the bucket. "Onward, to adventure!" she said.

The bog I lived next to was a blackberry bog, vines snaking throughout the entire peninsula and creeping up the alders and cedars scattered about. We wandered through the sweet August air, trampling through dry grass and trying to shake the melancholy of summer's Sunday off our shoulders. You had to be careful; if you didn't watch yourself you could walk right into the web of a spider. They spun their webs all around the blackberry bushes — large spiders the size of dollar coins that loved to crawl on your face given the chance.

For the majority of the year the blackberry vines only proved a nuisance for those of us who lived by the forest. In late summer, however, the thorny blossoms pupated into plump berries by the dozen. I spent my childhood picking them from this bog with my family. I remember running around with my brother, buckets in hand, and picking as many berries as we could find. Not many reached it to the bucket, though, and by the end of the day our mouths would be purple and sticky from juice. We would stay at the bog until the sky turned orange with evening, the crickets in full swing by that point. When we all would get home our mother would bake our bounty in a berry cobbler — the best part of summer far and wide. But before reaching home, we would have to make our way back through the woods and over the hill. This part I always hated.

Sometimes I dream about those evenings, walking back home with our buckets of berries. It's one specific dream, and it's not a memory. I am three years old and holding my tin bucket. My brother and father are ahead, hacking away at the brush with machetes. We are walking back uphill, surrounded by cedars and Douglas firs. The evening sky looks white behind the forest canopy, and I am waiting with my mother, pulling on her coat. I ask her to pick me up, and when she finally does I rest my head on her shoulder. I look behind my mother and see a pair of eyes, glowing green things peaking at me from behind a tree. I keep quiet, hugging my mother tighter. The eyes begin to rise, and something hisses at me. I scream.

I didn't tell Jill about my nightmare about the bog. I'm not sure why; she would've thought it was cool. But I didn't want her to know that part of me was still scared, all these years later. This was our last sleepover, but it was also a chance to get over myself, to make peace with the past. I was Jill's co-adventurer, not a coward.

The weather was warm enough for shorts. Jill led the way — as she always did. I missed my pants at the time. When I wore pants I didn't have to worry so much about ticks and stinging nettle. The blackberry bushes themselves could cut up your legs in a matter of minutes. Thorns lined up and down the twisting vines, and even the leaves were sharp. Was it worth it, though? Absolutely. At the ends of these vines were bushels of blackberries. I held one in my hand, this squishy, juicy thing, and chewed it in my mouth. I had forgotten what blackberries tasted like, it'd been so long.

Ku-plink, ku-plank, ku-plunk.

The sounds of fruit hitting the bottom of our buckets echoed throughout the bog. I could feel the sun's rays on my shoulders as I reached up for a cluster of berries, careful not to disturb any large spiders.

"Will the berries go bad if we leave them out overnight?" Jill asked. She stood deep in the center of a berry bush, surrounded on all sides and bleeding slightly from her legs. Standing on the fringes I could see that her bucket was already half-full.

I shook my head. "They'll be fine. We can cover the buckets at night so animals can't smell them."

"We should've brought a cooler," she said, and then winked at me.

My heart raced a little faster. "Next time." But there wouldn't be a next time.

We kept picking for another hour, Jill going the extra mile and myself taking extra care not to get scratched or disturb anything. My mouth turned purple by then — Old habits die hard. I looked down at my bucket to see I hadn't even half-filled it. Why did it feel as if Jill were ahead of me in everything? Why was I even comparing myself? I caught myself wondering if I resented her. Then I realized I had lost sight of her.

"Anita! Get over here!" There was a sense of urgency in her voice. I dropped my bucket, berries spilling all over the ground. I ran toward the noise. I had no idea what kind of trouble Jill was in, but I found myself ready to fight, adrenaline rushing through me. I ran through sticker bushes, my legs getting scratched and torn up as I did so. Where was she?

"Faster, Anita!" Jill wasn't far away. I could see her shape through some of the bushes ahead of me. I crashed through, thorns sticking to my clothes and ripping as they passed. Jill stood there, bucket in hand, giving me a strange look.

"Whoa," she said. I was bloodier than her. Jill's smirk turned into a laugh.

"Are you okay?" I asked.

She nodded. "Sorry, yeah, I'm fine. You look worse than I do!"

"Then what's wrong?"

Jill blinked at me. "Nothing! Nothing's wrong, dude. I just found something." She looked over to the left of me. There, embedded in the blackberry vines and almost melding into the landscape, sat the shell of a car — a vintage car, rusted and weathered away. The doors lay on either side of it, having fallen off the hinges. The windows were devoid of glass, smashed decades ago.

"Why is there a car here?" Jill asked.

"How should I know?" I said.

"I mean, you live here. You should know the history of this place."

I knew the area had been a logging site a hundred years before, and I knew all the trees on the hill were second growth. I didn't know much about the bog, though. The car looked as if it hadn't moved for ages. Jill stood on the hood and jumped up and down a few times. I wanted to tell her to get off, to let sleeping ghosts lie and not disturb this artifact. But mostly I didn't want her to get hurt. The car didn't belong here, hidden, dying under the vines. I wondered how long it would take for a car like that to rust into the shell of a memory it had become.

"Where do you think the owners went?" Jill asked. I didn't respond, and looked down at my bloodied legs instead. Warm, red liquid began to creep down from the scratches toward my white socks. I didn't do anything to stop it. I imagined the owners driving in the car when it was new: some happy 1960s nuclear family on their way to a picnic. A mom, a dad, a brother and sister. They pick blackberries all day but when the sun goes down they find their car's tires stuck in the peat-mud, or the son notices something in the water and inches closer to inspect. The sister screams for him to stop. She runs to get her parents but it's too late. Maybe the family never returns to the car at all. Or they left it here on purpose. This was a place where you left things.

"Anita?"

I looked up. Jill had stopped jumping. I swallowed.

"How many berries have you picked?" I asked. She looked at me, confused, and then pointed.

"Bucket's almost full," she said. It sat there next to one of the orange rear wheels, almost filled to the brim with purple. Jill jumped down from the car. Then she did something terrible: She looked at me. I could see the concern on her face I never asked for.

"Are you okay, dude?"

I didn't know what to say. I didn't have any words I was holding back; my mind just drew a blank. I stared out for a moment before nodding. "Yeah, just phased out for a bit," I said.

She laughed, grabbing her bucket. "Well, snap out of it, man! We can't be all mopey during our last sleepover!"

I faked a smile. "You're right."

"We should get back to home base," she said. She put her arm around me and led us back, and I prayed she wouldn't notice my face turning red.

Jill began work on her alarm system that night. She had apparently packed the necessary supplies to do so.

"I wasn't kidding when I mentioned doing this," she said. I tried to muster up a level of energy to match hers, but I was tired. I opted to go search for kindling instead. There was a burn ban on, but Jill disregarded it. This was our camping trip and we were going to get the full experience. I told her I would be back quickly, but I took my time.

I remember, or dream, of standing on the bog's shore with my brother. Our parents don't know we made it out here all by ourselves. We are preteens, and we still think the world is filled with adventure and untapped potential. My brother is trying to scare me by talking about ancient bodies they've found in bogs, perfectly preserved.

"They're always found super jacked-up, like with stab wounds or hung by a rope before their bodies got dumped in," he says. I stare down the dark water and peer. I know there's nothing staring back, but on the off chance there is — I want to scare it. Let it know I am not afraid. My brother isn't helping.

"Then the body stays under for hundreds of years and the peat in the bog doesn't let bacteria break the flesh down 'cause it's so acidic and —"

"Will you shut up?" I say.

He ignores me. "There's probably a bunch of bodies right here right now. Under the water," he says.

"You're full of shit." I've just started swearing when adults aren't around. Swearing still feels bold and dangerous, not yet oversaturated.

"If you're so sure there's a body in there then why don't you go find one?" I ask. He looks down at the water, scrunches his face. I think it upsets him more than it does me.

"Screw you," he says. I'm tired, and fed up with him. I'm not proud of this next part, but I push him into the water, hard. The dark liquid splashes up into the air. Bits and chunks of peat bob up to the surface around him. He has to kick to keep his head up; it's an instant drop and the water is deep.

"Bitch!" he screams at me, between his coughing fits. I laugh. "You suck," he says, and I laugh harder. My brother gets this look on his face, as if something's not right.

"I just kicked something," he says.

I snort. "Yeah, right."

"I'm serious!" he says. My eye drifts. There is something floating toward my kicking brother. A log. A very long log. Or an alligator. It looks like one of those floating reptiles you see on documentary footage of the Everglades, except the head is smaller and much farther away from the body.

"I keep kicking something really big, Anita," my brother says. The log drifts closer to him. I can see a familiar set of green eyes on its head. It's stalking him.

"Get out," I say.

"What if it's a body?"

I point to the log and shout: "Get out!" My brother turns; he sees the log. It raises its head out of the water, attached to a stretched, serpentine neck and filled with needle-sharp teeth. It hisses. My brother screams. I scream. It lunges, and I am running through the trees.

I never told Jill about this dream either. This place wouldn't control me any longer. We make things up to escape our realities. The sky was a violent orange by the time I got back with the kindling. Jill looked up.

"Dude, check this shit out!" She motioned all around us at her creation. Her alarm system was more intricate than I had imagined. Twine reached out in all directions, boxing us in by a ten-foot radius. Empty cans with holes poked into them hung from strings. The surrounding trees and stumps had been dragged into this scheme, as Jill had looped twine all around them. We had a clear view of the water — the same spot I dream of pushing my brother in — but it felt more secure inside Jill's alarm system. Part of me wondered if she was as scared as I was. Why else would she make this thing?

I nodded. "I see."

Jill chuckled. "Now we'll be extra safe tonight, alert if any monsters come creepin'!" she said. There was playfulness in her voice, but a hint of anxiety as well.

We managed to make the fire by the time darkness blanketed the ecosystem. I'd forgotten to bring chocolate, so Jill insisted we use blackberries for our s'mores instead.

"We can pick more tomorrow," she said, stabbing marshmallows with sticks. I smiled. Jill was always so inventive, much more than I ever was. And even though the idea of blackberries with marshmallows with graham crackers sounded disgusting, I admired her refusal to be set back by anything. She bumped my shoulder.

"Hey," she said, smiling. "I told ya to stop bein' moody." She held a stick with a marshmallow at the end for me.

I held it over the fire. "Sorry."

She laughed, reaching into her blackberry bucket and popping a berry into her mouth. We sat in silence, the fire cracking and hissing over the sound of distant crickets.

"I can't believe we found a car today," Jill finally said.

"You found a car."

"I mean, you're the one that brought me here, right? Nobody else brings me blackberry picking in spooky bogs, or any other adventures we've had," she said.

I snorted. My marshmallow was getting burned, and I blew on it.

"Well, there's no one else I'd explore the world with," I said.

Jill giggled again. "That's gay, dude." I laughed back, or at least pretended to. I watched Jill mush blackberries and melted marshmallows between graham crackers and chew them with berry-stained lips, her scratched legs flickering in and out by the fire's light, and swallowed my feelings again. There were other things I never told my best friend.

Something hit the water out in the darkness just then — a loud crack of a splash less than a hundred feet away. We bolted up.

"What the shit was that?" Jill asked. The thing moved, just barely visible in the moonlight, and sank under the water. I didn't know what to say. Memories mixed with dreams filled my mind, but I blinked them away and stayed in the present.

"That was a beaver," I said. "They splash their tails on the water when they get scared." Jill stared out into the darkness, shaking her head.

"Pretty big beaver," she said.

We didn't spend the night of our slumber party staying up late talking about boys. I didn't have any boys, and Jill had dated so many she didn't like talking about them anymore. The two of us slept side by side in sleeping bags in the tent. Despite her unease, Jill fell asleep in a matter of minutes, and I was left alone to dwell over my fictions and childhood memories and the curves of Jill's body and the fact that I can't discern reality from imagined scenarios. I am running through the woods, crying out. I almost stumble over my sneakers at the top of the hill and tumble through the brush. I'm ripping through foliage that cuts my ankles and shins — ferns, nettles, Oregon grape. I burst from the forest and slam my fists on our front door. My brother has fallen in and a monster ate him. I can barely say the words through my choked tears. My mother runs for the hill as my father carries me behind her. I cling to my father's jacket, begging my parents not to go back because I can't lose the rest of my family. My brother isn't there when we come to the bog's shore. My mother is screaming his name, but his body is never found. I tell them about the monster. I don't tell them how he got into the water. I am told what I saw never happened, that my brother was an adventurous boy who loved catching snakes and scaring birds and making forts who just one day made a mistake and drowned. I am told not to mention monsters, to never explore again. And after a few years, these are just dreams mixed with memories to cope with unsettling natures. Monsters are a figment of my imagination.

Monsters are defense mechanis —

Something knocked the bucket over outside. I didn't move. It must've been a raccoon or possum. That damn beaver. Something real that rummaged around in the nocturnal hours. A hiss. A reptilian, throwback sound from long ago that I didn't want to admit was actually happening. I turned over and slowly — oh, so slowly — unzipped the tent door just enough to see through.

Dreams are not memories, and memories are not reality. I held my breath and looked upon what was true.

The bucket moved in the moonlight, the snake-like neck I knew so well protruding from it. I tried not to breathe lest it look up at me. The neck connected to a short lizard body that stood just behind the thread of Jill's alarm system, never setting off a thing. I could hear a tongue lick against the bucket's bottom as it lapped up the last of the purple fruit. The neck was massive, at least twice as long as the rest of the animal, allowing it to eat our day's bounty while we slept.

But I wasn't asleep. I was watching my dream scavenge for scraps by the moonlight. My dream was a living thing.

"What the fuck is that?"

I looked over to see Jill, her eyes wide with fear and excitement, and before I could say anything I heard the bucket drop to the ground with a snarl, and when I looked back there was my monster: the creature I had made up when I was too young to know monsters didn't exist, and it stared at us, that monster, with those glowing green eyes, and grimaced, and I could see the needle teeth and lizard snout and a hint of recognition, and as I screamed Jill ran at it with fists, and it charged and I shut my eyes and screamed and screamed and with a crack on the side of my head everything stopped dead. I remember silence.

I dream of the next morning, opening my eyes and finding myself lying on the yellow ground. Dried blood cakes my hair, and I smell of grass and campfire. I blink and look around. The ground is covered in dark splotches. It is hard to tell if they are blackberries or flesh. The tent is empty and our sleeping bags are torn to ribbons, our final slumber party forever finished. I get up. The sky is pink with sunrise, the birds as loud as ever, and the waters are perfect glass.

I walk to the edge and look down into the dark abyss. But at this time of day — the very beginning — the sunlight hits the water just right, and I can see down to the peat floor in honey-golden rays. I peer. The water is filled with shapes,

Art by Samantha Breaux

shapes that are familiar and yet so remote. Because there are people down there, so many people, just lying at the bottom as if in slumber. I see loggers from the 1900s, their flannel stained tea-brown and peeling off in flakes and bits, and Chehalis gatherers from long before when the land was fresh and unraped. The '60s nuclear family sleeps, too, the mother and father's blond hair dyed a permanent red as they hold a firm grasp on the picnic basket together, and the children sit patiently side by side. A third child sits with them, my brother, with red, needle punctures around his throat. He looks exactly as I remember, at the bottom of this bog where I left him. And right under me, where I saw her fall in, lies the girl I love — staring out at me from the darkened waters of my dreams.

After You Moved to the Midwest

by

Katherine Van Eddy

For James

I.

You could name all the Northwest trees
tell their stories

from the hemlock's grooved bark
to the cedar's long, reddish strips

(used for canoes and diapers)
to the Douglas-fir cones, the mice inside.

You could make a frightened child
hold a reptile and smile

You looked to the mountain
bowed at the cove

And now you know how it feels to leave
and miss the place you called home.

Art by Jenni Prange Boran

II.

Even Chinook salmon
can't wait to leave their river

learn to breathe with salt
in their gills

even they, thick-fleshed and homesick,
follow the same stream home

a fierce fight in their tiny fish bones
push against water's pull

and in their final days
find a mate they knew as infants

until, exhausted and blissful,
they lay against stones

let the water ebb to the estuary
leaving their bodies to slip, sag

and waste away, broken into bits,
fed back to the universe.

Allium Makes One Wish Before the Shootout

by

Daniel Wolfert

Introductory Note from the Author

A few weeks before I began writing this story, I was listening to the radio and an old folk song called "Lily of the West" came on. In the song, some men fight over a pretty girl colloquially called "The Lily of the West" because of her delicate beauty. This irritated me because it implied the girl's only notable traits were her beauty and delicacy. The song did get me thinking, however, about what title I would want if I lived in a Wild West-style world and after much deliberation, the answer I came up with was "The Onion of the West." The following story is a result of that thought.

I. Hardy as They Come

He laughs, just like all the others, just as I expect him to.

"The Onion of the West?" he cackles. "What sort of Podunk name is that, boy?" I shrug.

"That's just what they call me," I reply, sliding my hands into my pockets. I rock back and forth on my heels. The sun glints off my gun holster. "I don't make the titles 'round these parts. I'm just the sheriff in Heaven's Bounty

"Ooh, I bet you is," he sneers, slipping his thumbs into his belt loops. As he does so, his holster glints, too. He smirks. "Ain't you a little young to be playin' sheriff, son?" I continue to rock back and forth on my heels. His smirk slips away. After a long moment of silence, he spits onto the ground, leaving a black tobacco stain on the dirt of Main Street.

"Folks call me Dirty Dog Akimbo," he growls, "But we're so far out in the middle of nowhere, I reckon you ain't got wind of me yet, ain't ya."

"And why do they call you Dirty Dog Akimbo?" I say all polite-like.

"'Cause I play dirtier than a dog in mud, that's why," he spits angrily, "an' you best keep that in mind when I stuff your chest full of bullets, boy!" I shrug again. He blusters. "Well, then, ain't ya gonna tell me why they call you 'The Onion of the West?'" I stop rocking on my heels.

"Some say it's 'cause I can make a grown man cry," I reply, a smile on the edges of my mouth. I kick the dirt and chuckle. "But I reckon it's 'cause onions are so dang hardy. See, Mister Akimbo, onions are tough. They just keep on coming back, no matter what hits 'em. They's one of the hardiest growing things on God's green earth." I grin at him all sly-like. "Guess the folk here reckon I is, too."

He scowls as I tip my hat to him.

"The name's Allium," I say, "and I'm as hardy as they come."

Photograph by Jeff Winner

II. Ain't No Lily

You wanna know what they called me 'fore I was the Onion of the West? I'll tell ya.

When I was just a young 'un, other kids used to call me "Lily of the West" — 'cause I had long hair, and was so small and was a bit of a dandy, I reckon. That changed when I was eleven, and Ma first taught me how to shoot. Had me shoot at cans sitting on the farm fence. Hit four outta six on my first try. Six outta six on my second. I was so dang good, she said I'd outdraw Sheriff Shoal by thirteen. By fourteen, nobody called me Lily of the West no more. I never told Ma or Pa about it — I didn't want them to see me get all ruffled. But at the age of twenty-six, I did tell Sheriff Perseid Falls.

He was the sheriff right before me, sent after the old sheriff, Shoal, retired. At four years older than me, he was the second-youngest sheriff we ever had — second only to me. I told him about it ten weeks after he arrived, one week before he would die.

"Well, don't that just sound like nonsense!" he said, sitting beside me on my toolshed. "You ain't no lily."

I grinned. "Well, I reckon I'm a bit of a dandy," I leveled, "Ain't that the same thing?"

"'Course you a dandy," Percy said, winking. "Else you wouldn't be here with me. But lilies ain't never had a use. Can't eat 'em, can't smoke 'em, can't chew 'em. Lilies are just there to look mighty pretty."

I punched his shoulder, laughing. "You saying I ain't pretty?"

"Allium Umbel," he said, rubbing his shoulder, "you are so much more than pretty. You're as hardy as you are sweet." He stopped rubbing his shoulder. One of his hands settled on my knee. "Why, I reckon you about the sweetest thing I ever did see," he said with a twinkle in his eye.

I blushed and looked down at my boots. "Reckon I feel about the same about you, Percy," I mumbled to them.

"Well, sweet heavens and hallelujah!" he shouted. "You just made me feel like every falling star I ever did see landed right in my outstretched hand!" I chuckled as he flung his hat into the air. He pulled me close. I felt his fingers on the nape of my neck. "Allium Umbel, I dub you the Onion of the West," he murmured, mighty gentle-like, "'cause you're as hardy and as sweet as an onion — and that is the Wry Whisky truth."

III. That Side of the Window

"How about we make this easy, then, Mister Allium?" Akimbo says. "You hand over two full bags of wishroot seed, and maybe I won't fill your body with enough bullets to stock a cupboard."

"Gee, Mister Akimbo," I say, placing a hand on my holster. "Did you think you was the first to come to Heaven's Bounty lookin' for some wishroot seeds?" His cheeks flushed. "You ain't the first, and you certainly ain't gonna be the last."

"You bet I ain't the last," he snaps, "but you can bet I'm gonna be the last you ever see!"

"Sure thing, Mister Akimbo," I say, all courteous-like, "but don't you think that was what all the others said, too?"

His blush deepens. He spits a black tobacco stain again. "Maybe, son, but you ain't never had nothin' but wastrels and vagabonds after your wishroot 'fore this," he says. "I been lootin' Podunk sheriffs a long time, and where are they now, boy?" He lifts his right foot slightly, and I know what he'll do next. "Six feet under God's green earth, ain't they?" And as he says this, he kicks up a cloud of dirt toward me, draws his gun and shoots. I lunge sideways behind a market stall just as his foot lifts. His gun fires long after I'm out of the way.

"Stop hidin' like a dandy, boy!" he roars, and fires into the market stall. The cabbages and carrots on it explode above me. "Ain't ya gonna fire back? Or are ya scared to face me?" His voice lowers as I hear him take a few steps toward the stall. "'Cause I would be mighty scared, if I was you."

"Cheatin' scoundrel!" Old Sheriff Shoal shouts from his window, and Dirty Dog Akimbo wastes a bullet in his direction. Shoal ducks down and it strikes the windowsill. "Men like you ain't got enough honor to fill a thimble!" he shouts from out of sight. Akimbo laughs, and I know why.

It's always the townsfolk talking about honor. About a sheriff needing it, about how it's all you got left when the fields are bare and the bottle's dry. About how I was picked sheriff after Percy 'cause that's what I got — honor, and the keenest eye for a gunshot this side of the Mississippi. But when the fella you love is staring down some nameless bandit coming for this week's wishroot harvest, there ain't no honor. When the fella you love is lying on the ground with a bullet in his gut, and all that's between you and that bandit is the gun in your hand, there's just killing or being killed.

What Shoal's really talking about is looks. What you look like when the townsfolk watch you from their houses, what you're gonna look like when they tell the story of your last shootout. When you're on that side of the window, it don't matter that in a shootout, all you can think is surviving. When you're on that side of the window, crying looks like cowardice, and desperation looks mighty coward-like. But honor never looks bad. Not honor. Never honor.

Honor sure looks mighty fine from that side of the window.

IV. As True as My Name

Ever wonder why the folk of Heaven's Bounty call it the "Wry Whisky truth?" I'll tell ya.

Folks say that, when the sands was young and the moon was just a sweet thing climbing outta her crib, a woman came walking these ways. She was full of wishing — wishing for a soft bed, wishing for a cold drink, wishing for her ma and pa now lost to the desert — and mind you, it ain't no easy thing to carry all that wishing around. Wishing is a mighty hungry business. Aside from her wishing, though, she didn't have nothing but the coat on her back, the bullets in her bandolier, her nag No Reins Riley and her own God-given name — Wry Whisky.

Now Wry Whisky had been traveling for many a day. Some say months, maybe years, but either way she was hungry enough to eat the moon and thirsty enough to wash it down with the Atlantic. She was just about ready to give up when outta the blowing sand and sun, she saw a green valley filled with constellations of purple flowers. Happier than a pig in mud, she and her nag stumbled forward and collapsed onto the dark earth. As Wry Whisky looked around, she realized the flowers were onion stalks.

Photograph by Jeff Winner

"Well, I'll be!" she cried to her nag, pulling a stalk up to reveal an onion bulb. Peeling away the tough skin, she took the first, sweet, sharp bite. She thought of her ma and pa. She thought of how she missed them. She thought of how she wished they were still with her. She wept.

Now, it ain't nothing special to cry when you eat onion. But folks say she cried so much and her tears were so full of wishing that all the onions of the valley drank it up. They drank up her wishes for a soft bed, and her wishes for a cold drink, and her wishes for her ma and pa lost to the desert. They drank up her tears and changed into something new and strange. They became the first wishroot on God's green earth, and as they did, they began to glow like stars.

Now, it ain't nothing special to cry when you eat wishroot, neither. Some say it tastes like the first time you ever been kissed. Some say it tastes like your mama hugging you when you was a little thing. Some say it tastes like every falling star you ever did see landing right in your outstretched hand, like honor from that side of the window and all you ever wanted. That's why the bandits come — Folks pay a fortune to taste wishroot, and double that to get a hand on wishroot seeds.

"Ain't this just like all of Heaven's Bounty, laid out on a silver platter," she laughed, "and ain't that as true as my name."

But Wry Whisky didn't know nothing 'bout that. She didn't know 'bout the house she'd build that would turn into a town, or 'bout the town folk naming it after her words, or 'bout the glowing onions that would one day be a something worth killing for called wishroot. What she did know was she was somewhere green and safe, in a valley of onions glowing like every falling star she ever did see.

V. Draw

"We playin' hide and seek now, is we?" Akimbo breathes as his footsteps get closer. I say nothing. He's ten feet away. "I knew I was drawing against a little boy, but I didn't think you was that young." Eight feet. "How about we play a different game, huh?" Five feet. "How 'bout cops and robbers?"

He leaps forward just as I stand and knock the stall backwards. He steps out of the way before it falls on him, but it gashes open his right shoulder as it falls. He yells. I whirl around to shoot, but even with the wound he draws faster, and I leap behind Carpenter Betty's wagon for cover.

"Clever, ain't ya?" Akimbo grunts, and he ain't playing now. "Well, you ain't the only clever one here." I hear his footsteps, then a huge grunt of effort as the wagon tips dangerously toward me. I leap back, and as it rocks away from me, I throw my weight against it. It teeters for a moment, and I hear Akimbo cursing as it falls toward him. He leaps out of the way. The wagon topples over. Akimbo fires two more shots at me, and I roll sideways so we're on opposite sides of the overturned wagon. It's large enough to lend us both cover as we crouch.

We raise our heads over the wagon. We look quickly from one another to the surrounding debris and back again. The overturned wagon is the only cover on Main Street now. If either of us stands or runs, the other will have an easy shot. We size each other up. We reach the same conclusion.

"Think you can draw faster than me, boy?" he says, so quietly I can barely hear it.

"Dunno, mister," I say with a little grin, "but we sure about to find out, ain't we?"

A slow, sly grin spreads across his face, too. His gun quivers in his hand. My gun quivers in mine. For a heartbeat, our only movements are the trembling of our fingers. A drop of sweat dangles from my left brow and falls. Old Sheriff Shoals' laundry sways in the wind. The townsfolk of Heaven's Bounty watch breathlessly.

We stand. We draw.

We fire.

VII. The Wry Whisky Truth

You wanna know the truth? I'll tell ya.

Truth is at the end of the day, a heart full of wishing has two choices: Eat the world, or eat itself. Either you work yourself to the bone every day farming or shooting or robbing, or you drown in the hopes you had for a wedding with Ma crying and Pa's rhubarb-wishroot surprise. Either you feast on the frost-kissed onions and the falling stars before you, or you feast on your own heart till you ain't got a wish left in this world.

Truth is that all being hardy means is learning how to starve your heart. All it means is learning how to not eat the world and not eat your heart and live with that empty plate. All it means is trying not to wish until the day comes you can't not wish no more.

Truth is all that wishing's gotta go somewhere. If you're a farmer, you put that wishing into next year's crop and the color of the sky at three a.m. If you're a sheriff, you put that wishing into a cowboy hat and a glinting badge on the chest of your jacket.

If you're a wishroot seed, though, it ain't the same thing. Maybe you're planted, and all the wishing running through ya turns into a bulb, a stalk, a constellation of flowers. Maybe you die, and that wishing goes back to the earth for another wishroot to drink up. But maybe you're not put into the ground, and mind you, wishing is a mighty hungry business, so all that wishing grows inside until it's damn well ready to burst. Until it changes you from a seed into something that don't know nothing but hunger. Until you could swallow up all of God's green earth.

But you gotta be fed wishes, whispered to you every night before bed. You've gotta soak them up, so you know what wish to grant when the time is right. And you've gotta be kept from sprouting.

Somewhere dark. Somewhere dry.

Like the inside of a gun barrel.

VIII. Planting Seeds

It looks like a supernova.

His gun goes off with a sharp bang. Smoke curls from the barrel. Sparks ignite the gunpowder. The bullet catches the sunlight. But I don't have a bullet in my barrel. Inside of my gun, pulsing with purple light, are six tiny wishroot seeds.

The one I fire shines like a meteor as it flies and in the space of a blink, it explodes. It becomes a mouth as wide and black as a moonless night. Dirty Dog Akimbo doesn't even have time to scream as it opens wide, swallows first his speeding bullet, then Akimbo's gun itself before vanishing. It's over in a moment — the gunfire, then the mouth, then me and my barrel pointing at Akimbo and the smoking space where his gun once was.

Silence.

"Now you best get outta here, mister," I say all quiet-like, "'fore the same happens to you." Akimbo sputters. He looks down at his hand. He looks up at me. He blinks in horror, then turns and runs down Main Street. I watch him get smaller and smaller as he disappears into the sands.

The townsfolk burst into applause, cheering and stamping their feet. They flood onto Main Street, hugging one another and clapping me on the back. I grimace.

Later today, Old Sheriff Shoal will help me fix up Carpenter Betty's wagon. If there's still time, we might get started making a new market stall, too. Funny thing is, when it's all cleaned up, this town won't remember. It'll be just another time the Onion of the West outdrew a bandit. And they won't think about it until another one comes after those seeds, hoping for a taste of everything they ever wished for.

It's an ugly thing, I won't deny it. And it sure leaves a mighty fine mess in its wake. But wishing's a mighty hungry business, and sometimes, that's what wishing looks like — a mouth so big it would swallow all of God's green earth if it could.

That's just the way it is — and that's the Wry Whisky truth.

Good Things

by

Kristy Gledhill

It's a good thing there are cats in this world

To take the place of another cat

whom you loved so much

Because he understood what you meant

and what you needed,

and exactly where to poop,

and how much you loved him,

but who disappeared

and who may or may not have been chewed by a coyote,

or tangled with a raccoon

or taken home and kept

by the idiot who can't read your signs pleading for his return.

You just don't know.

And it's a good thing there are

painfully shy and sensitive young men

and their batshit-crazy grandfathers who

take care of dozens of cats in houses

where you can go, say, on a Saturday afternoon

and pet said cats for hours and pick out one or two

For your very own.

"Maybe you'll go home with three!" he says with a maniacal laugh.

But you think then you would be disqualified from bariatric surgery,

should you ever need it,

according to Emily.

Three cats is one too many

To prove you're sane enough to have your stomach stapled.

Good thing your internal filter

is still intact enough to keep this fact to yourself

while you pet alllll the cats

It's also a good thing you found two cats that day

To take the place of your one, beloved friend Geordi –

Named after Geordi La Forge on Star Trek

not because he was black, which is what everyone thought,

but because he was friendly and smart and curious.

And finding two cats is a good thing not just because

"Look! I found some awesome cats to replace my old cat!"

But because that's the night he came over

and snuggled on the couch with you

and then broke up with you,

saying you exhaust him,

mentioning the fact that sometimes

you sleep on the beach, out under the stars, and that's dangerous,

saying you are "celestial," out there,

that you dip your toes in the terrestrial world ten percent of the time,

which is exactly what someone who

"Lives in the terrestrial world ninety percent of the time"

would say, isn't it?

He's measured it.

Anyway, you have the cats.

You don't have him.

And that sucks,

but already they love you,

and you felt it coming,

And he had his issues, believe me.

It's also worth noting that

it's a good thing there are places like Nisqually

where on a Monday afternoon

after the breakup

before you start a new job

and sort of have to have your shit together,

you can set out on a meditative walk, at a good clip,

and head out into the reach on a boardwalk

that is nailed tight and doesn't squeak or sway,

out over the "dangerous soft mud" and low-tide ebb.

And you can walk your ass off out into the Sound

to the incessant beat in your head, your body,

and finally reach the end and look out over the delta

at the place where everything has happened in your life:

relocation, physical healing, dissolution, bravery, treachery,

happiness, depression and discovery –

and stand there motionless after a long walk,

face to face with the teeming delta and silent islands

and feel the tears course down your cheeks.

And it's a good thing this place is so near Olympia,

where an aging hippie can show up out of thin air

and hear you sniffling and see you wipe away tears and wait

and say, "Do you need an ear?"

And she means it and she quotes the Buddha

and you end up sitting cross-legged on a bench with her

talking about suffering and detachment

and you realize your issues are the world's issues,

and on this day four years ago,

the aging hippie spread her dear husband's ashes at Lake Shasta.

And you don't ask her name

and she doesn't ask yours,

but you leave her with a long hug,

complete with "mmmmm"s and bows

and she says, "I just know you're a bodhisattva"

and you squeeze her shoulders and give her a long look goodbye,

trying to see her eyes through her dark shades

and are off again,

walking, solving, resolving, opening, crying, smiling, laughing,

thinking, thanking the universe for good things.

Art by Scott Hammond

The Fears

by

Sammy Vickstein

Slowly, he ascended the stairs to the attic. He did not walk by sight but felt his way with his right hand resting on the wall, his feet finding firmness after each searching step. There were always too many stairs, more than made any sense.

From somewhere behind, his sister called, "Where are you? I'm hungry!"

He did not want to feed her. His left shoulder smarted in response. He stood still and held his breath.

She began to climb the stairs. He felt each step reverberate through the wood from her to him. He shuddered. If he kept climbing, she could not catch up to him before he reached the attic, but then she would find out. So he set the key and unlit candle on the step he had reached this time, set them in the dark corner of the right wall where he would remember and hopefully no one else would stumble upon them.

"You're not supposed to be up there," she reminded him.

"I'm know. I, I thought I heard the cat up here," he called down as he descended the stairs.

"I don't want the cat."

"No, you don't," he answered, and his left shoulder sang with pain.

She wanted to play after dinner but her brother would not cooperate. Angered, she demanded her father make him play.

"Better let him rest now, hon. Besides, I need help putting up a new wall outside. Would you like to help?" Her father asked.

"No," she muttered.

"Great! Grab your coat!" her father answered.

He had a way of clarifying that a request wasn't a question.

They already had six circular walls surrounding their house.

"Why another one?" she asked as she held a plank of wood in place for her father.

"You're too young to be afraid," he answered, "but don't worry, you'll learn."

He found putting up the walls was exhausting: the constant checking for cracks and filling them, the putting up of new walls when the cracks revealed too much. But more exhausting than all this were the fears fueling the construction. He was the only one in the family who took the fears seriously. Rather than a manageable weight to be shared between his wife, their children and himself, it was all on him. As they had no desire to share the burden, he tried not to take it out on them. He really did try.

The father went back inside the house as darkness set. Three hours of work. Two and a half hours more than his daughter. He poured two glasses of whiskey, but his wife's ghost would not join him this evening.

She was in her son's room.

She watched him sleep as blood from fresh wounds stained his sheets.

The ghost worried about him. She couldn't help him in concrete ways anymore. He wasn't very strong; he never could stand up to his younger sister. She was particularly worried about his determination to reach the attic. That would ruin everything.

He had always felt closest to his mother. His

Photograph by Ric Colgan

father was too preoccupied with fortifying the home to be any use inside it. And his sister sucked the life right out of him. His mother cared. Had cared. In some strange way, still did? And if she were around, she'd understand.

If he could only get help, his father, maybe even his sister could still be saved. It was this house. Something bad. Something suffocating. Living, almost. And he knew his father knew. Early on, his father would tear down a new outer wall the day after putting it up. The boy would watch from inside as his father lifted the sledgehammer in a motion that should've been effortless for such a strong man and struggle as if he were swinging underwater. Fighting some elemental force, a natural law. The next day he would put the wall back up and begin to build yet another. Eventually he gave up the demolition, but he still knew.

The boy's sister hadn't always been such a terror. They had been friends once, before this house.

But that was a very long time ago. Such a very long time.

Leaving Bisbee

by

Leah Mueller

"I like your outfit," I said to the inebriated cowboy. We stood together at a long, wooden bar and stared at gleaming rows of bottles on the mahogany shelf. The interior of the Bisbee Stock Exchange was cavernous and spooky, filled to overflowing with the ghosts of real cowboys. After 125 years of continuous operation, the establishment effortlessly retained its air of Wild West authenticity. My companion was middle-aged and lean, with long, gray hair and a handlebar mustache. He sported a checkered, western shirt, tight jeans and shiny boots with spurs.

I was flattering him, as his look struck me as an absurd cliché. Bisbee was the sort of town where city officials paid guys to dress up like cowboys and lounge on the museum steps. It was a calculated tourist gambit, designed to inspire folks to purchase Kokopelli key chains and leather wallets embossed with rodeo scenes. The locals despised the tourists but were utterly dependent upon their revenue.

"I hate it when people say that shit," the cowboy replied. He leaned across the bar like a cartoon of himself, placed his hat on the counter. "I don't dress like this to impress people. These are my clothes." He picked up his shot glass, took a huge gulp, and stared at me angrily.

"I'm sorry," I said, hoping to assuage his ego. The cowboy waved his hand dismissively. Let me buy you a drink," he offered. "I'm used to this sort of bullshit. I get it all the time." I settled into my barstool and ordered a pint of Electric Dave's. The brewmaster had recently been sprung from prison after serving time for a marijuana-smuggling conviction. The locals didn't care what he did, they loved his beer so much. It was easy for me to see why. Electric Dave's was an excellent brew, smooth and hoppy and worthy of its name.

"That Dave sure is an operator," the cowboy muttered. A buxom, leather-faced bartender shoved a glass in my direction, then turned her attention to other matters. "I don't know how he manages it. There are folks in this town who make it and others who don't. You have to know whose asses to kiss. I don't kiss asses, but I've kicked a few. I've had my ass kicked too, more than once. Know what I mean?"

I took a thoughtful sip from my beer. My companion had summed up the human experience pretty well. "Best you can do is hope for a 50/50 split," I said.

The cowboy nodded appreciatively. "My name's Rick," he said. "I think we're going to get along."

I accepted a shot of Maker's Mark from the bartender. Rick gazed at the contours of my body, then looked away quickly. For the first time, I noticed a pile of fresh rosemary on the counter beside him. He had arranged the sharp little branches on an unfolded napkin, and they gleamed slightly in the pale bar light. "I picked it in a nearby field," Rick explained. "I can't resist the stuff." He held one of the sprigs under my nose and I sniffed deeply. "I'm going to dry it when I get home," he said. "It's really good in bread."

I thought of my own home, fifteen hundred miles away in Tacoma. My live-in partner and I separated several months beforehand, after my mother died and left me with one-quarter ownership of her Bisbee four-flat. Mom's building had been a miners' boarding house for many years. She paid cash for it, resurrected the rock garden and died a few years later.

The local real-estate market was slow and the building had taken a year to unload. As a result, I was no longer on speaking terms with my siblings. They had objected strenuously to my decision to sell the place. I'd flown to Arizona to tie up emotional loose ends and collect my $19,000 share. That was a miserable year, 2000, and I was eager to shake the dust of the Bisbee curse from my bones.

Rick gestured toward the bartender and two more shot glasses appeared in front of us. I sipped my amber liquid eagerly. Rick chugged his drink and signaled for another. "Why are you in town?" he asked.

"My mother's house finally sold," I explained. "She lived half a mile away. I'm here to say goodbye since I won't be back again."

"You'll be back," Rick said. He drained his glass and a new one arrived. "Get her one, too," he told the bartender. The woman hesitated, then shuffled across the bar with an air of resignation and measured another shot. She placed the glass in front of me and turned away quickly. I gazed at the tin ceiling. Its geometric patterns swirled and melted into each other. The sound of raucous laughter rose from the street, then subsided. I suddenly felt queasy and realized I was quite drunk.

Perhaps a trip to the bathroom would help. I rose unsteadily from my stool and smiled at my new friend. "I'll be right back," I assured him. My feet shuffled toward the rear of the bar while the top of my body undulated like seaweed. I found a door that said "women" and wandered inside. After swaying on the toilet for several minutes I returned to the bar. Rick was nowhere in sight and the pile of rosemary was gone. Maybe he tired of our conversation and decided to go home. I couldn't blame him. In my current state of mind I was probably terrible company.

Art by Amber McLean

The men's lavatory door opened and Rick wandered into the room. He staggered for a moment but quickly righted himself. With feigned casualness, he sauntered over to his barstool. Rick gave the counter a sideways glance, and a stricken expression came over his face. "The rosemary!" he cried. "It's … gone! Somebody must have stolen it!"

"That's ridiculous," I replied, shaking my head. "Who would steal rosemary? It grows wild in these parts."

Rick's eyes became suddenly wet. "People are no goddamned good," he said bitterly. "You never can trust them to do the right thing." He blinked back tears and shook his head. "They snatched it after I went to take a leak. This town is full of backstabbers."

I could imagine better ways to stab a man in the back than stealing his rosemary but didn't say so. My own experiences in Bisbee had been less than ideal. Over the years, two different men dealt me cruel rejections — a junkie writer carrying on with a local barfly, and a confused drummer who kept divorcing and remarrying his wife. It was exactly the sort of town that inspired wild-herb theft.

"You have to trust people anyway," I said. My voice sounded compassionate yet firm, as if I actually believed the words. I drained my shot and Rick waved down the bartender, ordered two more. I continued relentlessly, "I mean, they don't deserve it, but what choice do we have?"

For the first time, Rick stared directly into my eyes. "I don't know," he said. He looked away, embarrassed. "It's my own fault for letting people screw me over. I never learn."

"That makes two of us," I assured him. I pivoted on my stool and grabbed the edge of the bar so I wouldn't topple. My empty glasses glistened on the counter. I had managed to set a new personal record of a beer and five shots in less than two hours. I strongly suspected I wouldn't be proud of this record when morning arrived. "I'd better go back to my hotel," I said apologetically. "Thanks for the drinks. I enjoyed talking with you. I hope you find more rosemary."

Rick fixed his eyes on my body, then looked away sharply as if seized by pain. "You're really attractive," he said. "I'm going to go home and masturbate." His tone was morose, yet philosophical, like he was resigned to a future of onanism. My sudden departure was deeply disappointing and came swiftly on the heels of the rosemary theft, but he would deal with both issues as well as he could.

It was easily the most pathetic pickup line I'd ever heard. I emitted an uncomfortable laugh, and Rick set his jaw. "It's true," he insisted.

"I don't doubt it," I replied. Steering my body as if it were a ship, I labored my way toward the exit. A gust of wind caught my skirt, and I clasped the edge of the fabric with one hand. The door whooshed shut behind me as I stepped onto the darkened sidewalk.

I couldn't remember the location of my hotel, and this made me furious. Nevertheless, I walked purposefully down the cobblestone streets, as if I knew exactly where I was headed. I'd figure out the direction as I went along, as I'd done many times before. There was no reason to hurry. I owned plenty of time. No one could steal those minutes from me. I'd plug them a good one before they had the chance. They wouldn't dare mess with me again.

I found my hotel and collapsed into bed. After several hours of fitful sleep, I awoke with the sun in my face. It beamed mercilessly into my eyeballs, and I winced as I raised myself from the mattress.

I wandered into the tiny bathroom and splashed cold water on my face. My ravaged, puffy-eyed reflection stared back at me from the mirror. I felt terrible, but not half as bad as I'd expected. At least I could drive to Tucson, drop off my rental car and hop a flight back to Seattle.

A cup of coffee would do wonders for my equilibrium. I left the hotel, wandered down the sidewalk toward the coffee shop. Finally, paper cup in hand, I drifted across the street toward the museum. Rick perched on the top step with his long legs dangling beneath him, waiting for the tourists to arrive. His face was expressionless as he stared at the horizon. The man fit his inscrutable cowboy role perfectly. When he spotted me, however, he ducked his head with shame. "I'm sorry," he muttered.

I shrugged. "Don't be," I said. "I'm not upset. It was a good talk."

Rick lifted his head and looked relieved. "Okay," he agreed. "I still feel stupid, though."

"How did you sleep?" I asked.

Rick's face brightened. "Oh, I never have trouble sleeping. My place on Chihuahua Hill is so beautiful. I always wake up at sunrise. You should come over and see it tomorrow."

You had to hand it to Rick: Although he kept losing, he never accepted defeat without a fight. "I'm flying back to Washington this evening or I'd say yes," I said politely.

Rick looked momentarily saddened, but then smiled. "Another day," he said. "You have to come up next time you're in town and watch the sunrise. I make a hell of a good breakfast."

I wasn't sure how to explain to Rick that I never intended to return to Bisbee. In less than an hour, I would climb the winding hill in my rental car, take one last look at the town and head toward the Tucson airport. The chilly, damp air of the Pacific Northwest would be a huge relief after the desert heat. "I'll look you up," I promised. "Take care of yourself."

Rick reached out his hand and I shook it firmly. His fingers were warm inside of mine and lingered there an extra moment. The poor guy needed every bit of warmth he could get. I released his hand and turned away, began my trek back to the hotel. Two packed bags rested beside the bed, waiting to leave Arizona forever. My departure couldn't come soon enough. The desert was a barren land of desperadoes, and I needed to make a timely escape. Otherwise, I might end up like them, and I would rather die than allow that to happen.

Before Gaddafi
by
Josie Turner

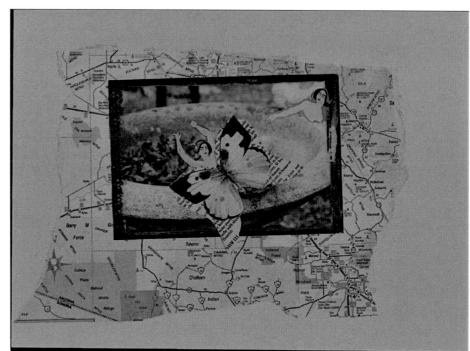

Art by Kristen Orlando

Before Gaddafi I put out my thumb to the air ...
I thought of Tom Joad. Leptis Magna
I said and my driver nodded.
The desert looked yellow and dry,
just as my scalp does now.

I needed to kiss civilizations
before me. What does humanity
do to destroy? Does preservation
mean burial in sand?

I slept under Severus' Arch.
In this solitude, my head heard
sounds of Hanoi scream
out of my Navy sack. Yet,

in the distance, like my mother's
lullaby, a single horse's neigh
nudged my nerves, gave me nectar,
let me lie still, almost touch
shooting stars.

Art by Kristen Orlando

Tunis

by

Josie Turner

Where is human stench, sewage, spoiled food?
An hour before Baç Liêu, on our ship, we could smell it.
But here … here. Blue and white buildings, cranes, horns, scooters.
Does sound travel faster than smell? Sweetness. Turmeric.
Perfume, spice could boil my blood once on land.

I had one bag. I wandered beyond docks.
I could not kiss her black, black eyes; her red, oiled skin.
I kissed her father's copper pots and the Souk
wound around me like a medic's gauze.

It's Sometimes Too Late

by

Jeffrey Winner

Richard stood on the front porch of his house and looked across at his neighbor's property. He shook his head in disbelief and cursed under his breath as he wondered how anyone could keep such an unkempt yard. Richard's lawn was green, lush and well-tended, whereas Stanley's was a brownish, weed-infested embarrassment.

The two old men lived side-by-side in a suburb of Philadelphia. A four-foot-tall, chain-link fence was all that separated their small plots of land. Over the many years they had been neighbors, Richard and Stanley typically made it only a few days before an argument over something trivial erupted.

Richard would harass Stanley to have his dog's waste picked up because the offensive smell wafted into his yard. Stanley would tell Richard to "put a clothespin on your nose and stop crying about it." The two were stereotypical grumpy old men. They drove each other crazy and had argued over the fence for decades, but not once did either of them ever consider moving.

It was a crisp and chilly September morning as Richard sipped his coffee and looked over the neighborhood. He sat on his favorite chair with legs crossed and a folded newspaper resting on his thigh. Just as he started to enjoy the quiet of the early morning hours, he was startled by the obnoxious sound of Stanley's automatic garage-door opener as it struggled to lift the heavy door. The rusty, old, metal springs wailed in a high-pitched screech that echoed up and down the street.

After what seemed like an eternity to Richard, the door came to a stop, and out shuffled Stanley in his slippers and loosely tied robe. Richard took one look at him and scoffed. "Jesus, Stan, close that robe, your saggy balls are about hanging out and families live on this street. And dammit," he continued, "why don't you put some lubricant on those springs and stop waking the entire neighborhood?"

Stanley, unaware he was being watched as he hobbled down the walk to retrieve his newspaper, turned and saw Richard sitting on his porch. "Put in some earplugs and stop crying about it, Dick," Stanley replied in a gruff voice. He turned and continued on his mission, seemingly unfazed by the early-morning interaction with his pain-in-the-ass neighbor. Richard fumed because he absolutely hated how Stan always said the name "Dick" with an obvious undertone.

"Would it kill you to let your grandkids do some chores for you?" Richard shouted after Stanley.

"You would like that, wouldn't you, Dick?"

"Now what the hell is something like that supposed to mean?"

"That's for me to know and you to find out," Stanley said, snickering.

"Oh, for Christ's sake, do you always have to be so childish?"

When Stanley arrived at the end of the walk he slowly stooped to retrieve his morning paper. Once in hand, he turned and began the arduous task of walking back to his house. He desperately hoped to make it inside without another word exchanged between his nemesis and himself — but he would have no such luck. At only ten feet from the garage, Richard called out again. "You know your house is becoming the eyesore of the neighborhood!"

Stanley replied, "After all these years of knowing me, Dick, do you really think I have one cell in my body that gives a damn about what these people think?" He waved his hand at the other houses.

"How about what I think?" asked Richard. "I have to look at that every day!" He pointed at Stanley's house.

"There is nothing wrong with my house!" snapped Stanley.

"For heaven's sake, Stan, look at all the paint peeling off it!"

"Well, if you don't like it, Rick-o, then feel free to come on over and paint it!" Stanley raised his voice. "And don't you have anything better to do than watch an old man limp down his front walk, waiting to see if he falls and breaks a hip?"

"Oh, don't be a wise guy," Richard replied forcefully. "As much of a pain in my ass as you are, I don't wish anyone a broken hip."

Richard scoffed again as he stood from his chair and crossed the porch. He leaned on the railing and prepared to lay into Stanley for being such a miserable asshole. But Instead of sending an opening volley of expletives toward his neighbor, Richard felt a searing pain shoot to his fingertips. He grabbed his left arm.

Stanley knew the signs of a heart attack well, having suffered three of his own. When he saw

Richard clutch his arm in pain, he shouted, "Hang on, Ricky, I'm calling an ambulance!" and rushed into the house as fast as he could. He fumbled the phone with shaking hands as he dialed 9-1-1.

Outside, Richard fell to one knee and labored for breath. The pain was incredibly intense as he waited for the end to come. It was a terrible feeling to believe these were his last moments on earth. He had only one thought, and it repeated in his mind over and over: "Any second now, it's gonna be lights out."

When Stanley returned from calling for help, he saw Richard sitting on the porch with his back against the railing. Richard was having serious trouble breathing and the pain in his chest and jaw grew by the second. The fear and anxiety he felt was overwhelming, and it only compounded his already-desperate situation. Even when bullets were flying and mortars were landing around him in Vietnam he wasn't as scared as he was now.

When Stanley finally made his way to Richard's side, he said, "Here, Ricky, put these in your mouth and chew." In his palm were two aspirin. "They're gonna taste like shit, but could save your life."

Richard opened his mouth, and Stanley fed him the bitter tasting pills. In the distance the faint sound of a siren began to grow closer. "You hear that, Ricky?" said Stanley. "The ambulance will be here in no time at all."

Between labored breaths, Richard replied, "Of course I hear it … After all … I'm not nearly … as deaf as you … you old bastard."

Stanley laughed out as he sat next to Richard and waited for help to arrive. "Even as death is knocking on his door," said Stanley, "my stubborn brother is standing in front of the Grim Reaper in defiance just like when we were kids. You always had to do things your way."

As the siren grew closer, Stanley closed his eyes and became lost in the flood of memories that filled his mind. He thought of the many great times he and Richard had shared together — the vacations with Mom and Dad in national parks all over the

Art by Amber McLean

country, the summers they chased girls and drank too much, their marriages, children, grandchildren, jobs and cars and all the gains and losses.

Stanley grew overwhelmed by guilt for the way he had always baited and fought with his brother. He turned his head and began to speak the words of an apology, but Richard's eyes had closed and he was no longer breathing. Unwilling to let his brother go without a fight, Stanley positioned him on the ground and began to perform CPR.

He pushed as hard as he could on Richard's chest for only thirty seconds before he, too, was gasping for breath. As the ambulance turned the corner and its siren pierced the quiet street, Stanley felt a sudden, sharp pain in his jaw, followed by the sensation of someone sitting on his chest.

When the ambulance came to a quick stop in front of Richard's house, the paramedic jumped out, grabbed her gear and climbed the porch stairs quickly. When she reached the top, she saw two old men lying side by side, holding hands as they drifted together into the silent darkness of death.

Dearest the Shadows

by

Samuel Snoek-Brown

All my nights here have been restless. Partly it's these damned hotel pillows — they're too flimsy, more rags than cushions. Also, I've been dreaming a lot. The first night at the conference, just into the hotel room and asleep in my clothes, I dreamed I was an animal wrestler, like bears and crocodiles, like at a country carnival. In the dream, I wrestle big dogs, Newfies and wolfhounds. I'm wearing one of those muscleman unitards from the '30s and keep thinking I ought to feel embarrassed but I realize no one in the audience even knows me. And of course you aren't there, either, which is somehow the greatest relief and the greatest sorrow. I wish you could see me, in all my ridiculous forms. Near the end of the wrestling match, I get into the dirt ring with a giant poodle as big as a pony and I'm hugging it, burying my face in its curled hair like wool, like a stuffed animal, but it sinks its teeth into the back of my neck and I wake with a migraine.

The night after that, I dreamed you died but I didn't realize it for a whole day. I bring you coffee in bed and it goes cold and I pour it into the freezer trays for iced coffee later. I run errands in a too-small car I drive down unfamiliar streets; what I'm looking for I don't know. When I come home, the house is dark and I call out for you and I think I hear you answer but it's from far away, as if you shut the bedroom door. I go to check and finally realize you've been dead the whole time, your eyes open and drying in the dark. Your lips are parted just a little, as though that's the way you escaped yourself.

My grandparents have a portrait of their grandparents, taken in those earliest days when it wasn't even photography but something metallic, a tableau burned into tin, the image shimmering in a weird, silvery light that goes black when you turn it the right way. In the dream, I remember this photo, and I remember the people in it were dead. A thing people used to do. My grandmother's grandfather rigid in a chair, his wife propped up by a mannequin stand. Their eyes eerily bright because they'd been painted on. There's a blur on the floor between my great-great grandfather's knees; my grandmother says it was the family dog come running into frame during the session.

In the dream, I see you dead in the bed and I make a decision. I get your makeup from the bathroom and paint your eyes, your lips, your cheeks. You used to ask me to paint your toes but I was hopeless at it, polish clear off the cuticle almost to your knuckles, but in the dream I am an artist. Fine lines along your eyelashes, a faint blush in your cheeks. When I do your lips, you almost seem to be smiling. I close your eyes for the eyeshadow and can't bring myself to open them again. Then I light candles in the dream, arrange them on the dresser and place a mirror behind them, staging the scene, all this natural light aimed at your pillow. I lie on the bed beside you and aim the phone, take selfies with you. Me kissing your face. Me sticking my tongue out. Me smiling at the camera, and when I time it so the wavering candlelight catches your lips just right, you're smiling, too, though of course I caught you with your eyes closed.

In the dream, I sit in bed flipping through the photos, a rapid montage in all these shifting colors from the candlelight, your face prismed through the phone screen into a whole spectrum of faces, and somehow I've forgotten you're dead. I've forgotten you're lying there beside me. I try to remember what I've been doing all this time, where you've been, where you are now. I try to look at your place in the bed beside me but can't seem to turn my head, and I start to panic like my spine has fused and I'm going to be paralyzed, and I need you to calm me down but I don't know where you are and as part of me begins to realize this is a dream and I start to wake up, the rest of me is swiping at your face on the screen of my phone, trying to drag-and-drop you out of digital space into the bed, but whenever I swipe at your image it scrolls left, flipping through photo after photo, past the ones I'd taken of us in your death and into other selfies — us on the beach, us at a bar, us on a mountainside — and your face gets less and less distinct in each photo and mine does, too, until I can't really make out either of us anymore. We are just colors and shapes made from light.

And then I woke alone in this hotel. There were voices in the hall, a maid, I think, and also some kids staying here for a basketball tournament. It took me a long time to realize I was awake, a long time to realize I wasn't breathing. Somewhere those two realizations got mixed up and I began to wonder if I was still dreaming, if this time I was the one who was dead. When the maid knocked on the door and called "Housekeeping!" I wasn't sure how to reply, and when she opened the door and pushed in her cart I was still lying in the bed, caught like a secret lover. Alone.

The third night of the conference, I stayed out with colleagues and drank too much and at some point got talked into smoking half a pack of cigarettes, and I slept hard and fast and woke with no memory of any dreams, just a sun behind my eyes and lichen on my tongue. Somehow I'd gotten so tangled in the bedclothes I had to disinter myself from sheets and blankets, those thin pillows slipping off the bed. They didn't make any sound when they fell to the floor, and I was grateful for that.

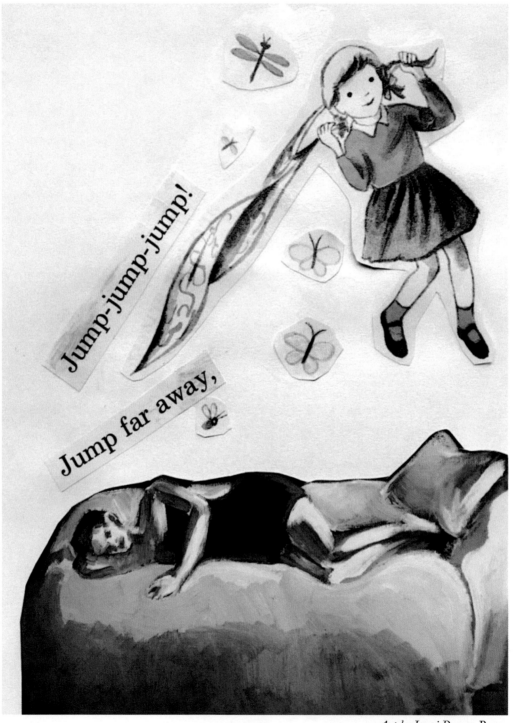

Art by Jenni Prange Boran

Last night, I dreamed I was back in Virginia with my cousin, carousing with a gang of his friends in the woods. We're twelve years old in the dream, the age I was when I last visited. My cousin tells me about this ravine, a rope some of the older kids strung to a high tree so they could swing out over the chasm, and the young me thrills at the hope of such adventure, but the dreaming me can already picture the rope swing because, as an adult, I remember it. We hike through dense fern-growth and over mossy knots of treeroot until we come to a massive trunk, wider than all of us together can reach around and so tall it disappears into the surrounding canopy. Bigger than it must really have been. There's the rope, as thick as my wrist, and everyone takes a turn swinging out. We're laughing and daring each other but after a while I notice our group has thinned — people who swing out don't swing back. I can't see where they've gone, if they've fallen or somehow landed on the other side. Then I see you.

In the dream, I'm still twelve, but you're an adult and I feel like one, too, and then I realize you're out over the ravine, and it looks like you're falling except you're not going down, you're away from the rope but still receding out over the empty space, into the ferns and underbrush across the ravine, and I grab the rope and swing out to catch you, trapeze-style, but you're too far gone, and I swing back. The only one not to disappear from the rope.

I woke in the night to the thin wheeze of the window AC, one of those flimsy, hotel pillows somehow flattened and wrapped over my head like a towel. I remember that time you fell asleep with a towel around your head and you slept so long the towel dried stiff so when you sat up in bed, the towel-turban held its shape. Like a ghost-you still lying there. How I laughed and arranged the blankets to look like you were invisible underneath them, and then I took a photo.

I lay awake in the hotel. Stared at the tiny, red light in the smoke detector and listened to the AC unit. Thought about that photo of the hollow towel-turban, of you without you, for maybe an hour. I thought about getting out of bed and wetting a towel, wrapping my own head, leaving it positioned on those flimsy pillows so I could take pictures of it with my phone. I wanted to evoke you, summon you into the void of a towel.

I could hear the cart in the hall, soft knuckles on neighbors' hotel doors, and I tried to remember which sign I'd hung on my door: Had I asked to be cleansed, or had I asked to be left undisturbed? I kicked loose the blankets, deflated pillows falling soundlessly, but then couldn't move any further. I could hardly breathe. I imagined how it would be if I fell back to sleep, how in dreaming again I might leave this room for somewhere else. The maid would enter and find me gone. Perhaps I was gone already and hadn't even realized it. Perhaps I was elsewhere with you, and you are laughing at me in a unitard, swinging on a vine, weightless as you watch me from the trees. The cart came closer. And I lay there still, the blankets a bundle at the edge of the bed, my bare knees bent, my arms splayed and my fingers in a hard grip on the bedsheets, afraid that if I tried to get up — to change the sign, wet a towel, pack my bags — my feet might not touch the floor.

Otis

by

Veda Leggett

Otis washed his hands, being particularly meticulous this evening. He carefully used the paper towel to turn off the faucet, then rubbed it with the towel until the chrome gleamed. He started to toss the towel in the trash but thought better of it, folded it neatly and tucked it into his pants pocket after using it to open the door into the hall. Humming tunelessly, he shuffled along the hallway to the office he left only moments earlier. The lights were on, the offices were empty and Otis felt he was the only one left in the whole world. He liked that feeling.

He walked around the desk, picked up the paper from the floor and carefully placed it on the desk. Stepping back, he scrutinized the desk closely. Yes, all was as it had been before he knocked the paper to the floor. The paper that sent him scurrying from the room. Things out of place always made Otis nervous. With a sigh of relief, knowing he had fixed everything, he moved away from the desk and resumed vacuuming. He did his usual thorough job and moved on to the next office: Baxter's office. Only one office and the employees' break room left and he would be finished for the night. He wanted to be done and out of here before the morning people came on. He didn't like anyone staring at him. He was working late but wasn't too worried. Doing a job that needed doing and doing it well was something on which Otis prided himself.

The first thing Otis noticed when he entered the break room was more copies of that same paper. Smiling to himself, he was happy he had been able to take care of something that evidently worried so many employees. He picked up the scraps of gift wrap lying around and wiped down the long table, stacking the papers on the end. Looked like someone had a going-away party. Fitting, he thought. The last thing he had to do was empty the trash, which he did. On the way out he stopped by the supply room and picked up some extra-large, heavy-duty garbage bags.

Otis struggled to load the oversize garbage can onto the bed of his sad-looking, old pickup truck, but he finally managed after much grunting and groaning. He leaned against the tailgate, pulled the paper towel from his pocket and wiped the sweat from his misshapen brow. He contemplated all he had accomplished in a short few hours and was proud. He may be ugly but he wasn't stupid, no siree. When he saw that article about Eldridge Baxter, one of the company's accountants, being a mutant, he knew he had to act. He had been angry and upset at first when he read the paper, then determined. Nobody else should be called "freak" and "mutant" like he was most of his life. Two mutants are one too many. He congratulated himself, happy he had knocked that paper off and read the article copied from The Onion. Otis tapped a goodbye to Baxter in the garbage can, climbed into his truck and drove off as the sun came up.

Photograph by Jeff Winner

Authors Featured in
Creative Colloquy Volume Four

(in alphabetical order)

Jonah Barrett

Jonah Barrett is a filmmaker, writer, and multimedia artist. His writing can be found in *Creative Colloquy, Everyday Genius, Lit.Cat, OlyArts,* and the bestselling Portland anthology *City of Weird.* He has worked as both a literary magazine and anthology editor, as well as journalist, actor, and art conservator. Someday a flying saucer will abduct him and his best friend.

Alec Clayton

Alec Clayton lives in Olympia and writes for the *Weekly Volcano, The News Tribune and OLY ARTS.* He's published eight novels. His latest is *Tupelo,* the story of a set of identical twins growing up in Tupelo, Mississippi in the 1950s and '60s.

Jonny Eberle

Jonny Eberle is a blogger, filmmaker, photographer and writer who lives in Tacoma with his wife and three typewriters. His previous short fiction was featured in *Creative Colloquy Volumes One* and *Three.*

Sean Michael Galvin

Sean Michael Galvin was born and raised in a small town in southeast Michigan, which proved to be the perfect breeding ground for the many anxieties and insecurities that he battles and writes about to this day. In the fall of 2016, he and his girlfriend moved to Tacoma from Brooklyn, New York.

Kristy Gledhill

Kristy Gledhill lives in Gig Harbor. She diligently tries and sometimes succeeds at presenting her true, authentic voice. After spending her childhood and young adulthood in Michigan, she's lived in the Puget Sound region for many years. There she worked for Tacoma nonprofits. She's a kayaker and hiker and has a cat named Ocho.

Aidan Kelly

Aidan Kelly has been writing poetry for 60 years. He has bachelor's and master's degrees in poetry writing from San Francisco State. He's had about three dozen poems published in journals over the decades. His collected poems are on Amazon with additional slim volumes of selected poems, and he's taught at the college level since 1979. He was an editor for Scientific American Books and Stanford University Press, and he has a wife, sister-in-law and three kids at home.

Veda Leggett

Veda Leggett is retired now, living in a retirement community and enjoying being able to devote her time to reading, writing and playing on her computer. She has three daughters who are excellent writers (one of whom has two middle-grade stories published) plus five grandchildren and three and a half great-grandchildren — One of her granddaughters is expecting a second child.

Leah Mueller

Leah Mueller is an independent writer from Tacoma, Washington. She's the author of two chapbooks, *Queen of Dorksville* (Crisis Chronicles Press) and *Political Apnea* (Locofo Chaps), plus two full books: *Allergic to Everything* (Writing Knights Press) and *The Underside of the Snake* (Red Ferret Press). She was a winner in the 2012 Wergle Flomp Humor Poetry Contest and a featured poet at the 2015 New York Poetry Festival. Her work has been published in *Atticus Review, Blunderbuss, Open Thought Vortex, Origins Journal, Outlook Springs, Quail Bell, Sadie Girl Press, Silver Birch Press, University of Chicago Memoryhouse* and many anthologies.

Linda Norlander

Linda Norlander has published fiction, humor and nonfiction regionally and nationally. Most recently, she had a short story printed in *The Bellevue Literary Review*. She was a finalist in the Tucson Festival of Books Fiction competition and is a guest writer for the Tacoma News Tribune.

Drew Piston

Drew Piston has been published via *The Gravity of the Thing, McSweeney's Internet Tendency* and *Shotgun Honey.* He lives on Vashon Island with his girlfriend, Ellen, and spends his time coding, reading, writing and playing music.

Samuel Snoek-Brown

Samuel Snoek-Brown teaches and writes in the Pacific Northwest. He's the author of the novel *Hagridden* and the flash-fiction chapbooks *Box Cutters* and *Where There Is Ruin*. He also works as production editor for Jersey Devil Press and lives online at snoekbrown.com. His work has appeared in *Bartleby Snopes, Fiction Circus, Eunoia Review, Red Fez* and *Timberline Review*. He received a 2013 Oregon Literary Fellowship and was shortlisted in the Faulkner-Wisdom competition, twice for short fiction and once for his novella. He was a finalist in the 2013 storySouth Million Writers Award and a 2015 contributor to the Sewanee Writers' Conference.

Justin Teerlinck

Justin Teerlinck is a forensic occupational therapist and creative writer who's had a humor column in *Whistling Shade* since 2008. He lives in Lakewood, Washington, having moved there in August 2016. The title of his story in this volume means "The Unicorn Hunters" in German.

Josie Turner

Josie Turner was inspired by stories her husband, William Turner, told of his overland journey from Tunisia to Tanzania in 1968 and 1969 upon his discharge from the navy and service in Vietnam. She hopes to bring contemporary meaning to the understanding of other cultures, the healing process of travel and the compassionate understanding of our veterans. From 2011 to 2013, she was honored to be Tacoma's poet laureate. She has a master's degree from the Rainier Writing Workshop at Pacific Lutheran University and teaches English and literature at Clover Park High School.

Katherine Van Eddy

Katherine (Kat) Van Eddy is a California-born poet living in Puyallup, Washington with her husband, two young children and a cat. She earned a bachelor's degree in creative writing and a master's in elementary education, and she taught for three years before staying home to take care of her kids.

Sammy Vickstein

Sammy Vickstein is a Tacoma writer who focuses mainly on poetry and stories. He likes to write about what makes him laugh, fear or continue to breathe, and he loves dogs.

Cathy Warner

Cathy Warner is a columnist, freelance editor and writing-workshop leader with a master's degree who's also a home renovator and realtor. In addition to her poetry volume *Burnt Offerings*, her stories and essays have been published in dozens of print and online venues. Find her at cathywarner.com.

Jeffery Winner

Jeffrey Winner was born and raised near Philadelphia and has lived in Tacoma, Washington for 15 years.

Daniel Wolfert

Daniel Wolfert is a composer, writer, avid reader, mediocre chef and terrible dancer based in Tacoma, Washington. He graduated from the University of Puget Sound with a degree in classical music and teaches voice and piano and working as a freelance composer in the South Sound area. When he was a child, he didn't believe there was a number larger than 100 and, to this day, he still has his suspicions.

Artist Featured in
Creative Colloquy Volume Four

(in alphabetical order)

Samatha Breuax

Samantha Breaux is literally too rad for this space marble. She graduated from the University of Washington in 2016 with a focus on microbiology, and her focus on science and the natural world consistently bleeds into her art. Her work has been featured in *Vanishing Point, Creative Colloquy* and the Olympia Zine Fest. One day a UFO will come abduct her and Jonah.

Jenni Prange Boran

Jenni Prange Boran is a writer and artist living in Tacoma. Her latest film, GLASS HOUSES, is in post-production in Vancouver, B.C. You can find more of her work at www.jenniprangeboran.com.

Ric Colgen

Ric Colgen is a local photographer in the Puget Sound area who enjoys creative portraiture, and scenic/artistic photography. He's always had a camera of some sort, often borrowed from family members when they weren't looking, and while he misses the creativity (and smell) of the darkroom, he has embraced the digital world wholeheartedly. He has been published, as well as released a self-published book of my work with local designers.

Carrie Foster

Tacoma artist Carrie Foster works in multiple mediums: graphite, inks, charcoal and gouache. She also makes paper, works in papier mache, sews and is a co-owner and designer for Tacoma art house screen printers Shroom Brothers. Drawing is her true passion. Going deep revealing the universal inspiration conduit within.

Scott Hammond

M. Scott Hammond is an artist, illustrator and graphic designer from University Place, Washington. He currently spends half his professional time designing hard goods for the tourist trade. His list of clients includes many national parks, museums and zoos. He spends the rest of the time toiling away on his detailed pen and ink illustrations. He works among themes of nature and fantasy. Scott also makes a pretty good Eggs Benedict, and he'll gladly make them for his wife. His two kids would rather eat pancakes, so he makes those too.

Amber McLean

Amber McLean is an artist with passion for all mediums. She discovered her love of art through an app called *Draw Something*, where she was recognized by artists around the world for artwork drawn using only her finger. She has since been commissioned to paint pet portraits, create custom diaper cakes, photograph senior portraits, teach and host paint parties. When she isn't in her studio, you can find her volunteering for her community through an organization she co-founded, Peace Out. Please find Amber on Instagram at @_mermaidamber or send her an email to giveartbyamber@gmail.com

Kristen Orlando

Kristen Orlando has been teaching English and Creative Writing in Tacoma Public Schools for 20 years. On school days, she can be found at the Science and Math Institute in Point Defiance Park. Her poems can be found in Creative Colloquy, Storm Cycle (kind of a hurricane press), and WA129, Sage Hill Press. Kristen loves to make "found" poems from other people's words and that has inspired her to make "found" pictures from other people's pictures. She would like to thank Jackie and Josh for this opportunity to see her pictures in print.

Bismark Pinera

Bismark Pinera is a tattoo artist and craftsman living in the Pacific Northwest. He has over 10 years of professional tattooing experience and has served as a guest artist in studios around the world, including Austria, Mexico, the Netherlands, Puerto Rico and prominent U.S. cities like Austin, Chicago, New York City, Seattle and San Diego. He continually works to expand his artistic craft and supports the local arts community and small businesses whenever possible. Recently, he's been collaborating with authors of the South Puget Sound to create meaningful artwork for quality books.

Jeff Winner

Jeff Winner is originally from Philadelphia, Pennsylvania and came to Pacific Northwest by way of the United States Army. He has worked in the photographic medium for over twenty years and has dabbled with art and the written world. He currently lives in Tacoma, Washington and spends much of his time with his three children.

Made in the USA
Middletown, DE
17 February 2022

61393989R00064